CHARLOTTE PERKINS GILMAN'S
# IN THIS OUR WORLD
AND UNCOLLECTED POEMS

CHARLOTTE PERKINS GILMAN'S
# IN THIS OUR WORLD
## AND UNCOLLECTED POEMS

*Edited by*

## GARY SCHARNHORST
## AND DENISE D. KNIGHT

SYRACUSE UNIVERSITY PRESS

Copyright © 2012 by Syracuse University Press
Syracuse, New York 13244-5290

*All Rights Reserved*

First Edition 2012
12  13  14  15  16  17       6  5  4  3  2  1

Excerpts from the Charlotte Perkins Gilman Papers collection are published with the permission of Schlesinger Library, Radcliffe Institute for Advanced Study, Harvard University.

"Supplement to 'A Conservative'" by Charlotte Perkins Stetson Gilman is published with the permission of Linda S. Chamberlin.

∞ The paper used in this publication meets the minimum requirements of the American National Standard for Information Sciences—Permanence of Paper for Printed Library Materials, ANSI Z39.48-1992.

For a listing of books published and distributed by Syracuse University Press, visit our Web site at SyracuseUniversityPress.syr.edu.

ISBN: 978-0-8156-3295-5

**Library of Congress Cataloging-in-Publication Data**

Gilman, Charlotte Perkins, 1860–1935.
  [In this our world]
  Charlotte Perkins Gilman's In this our world and uncollected poems / edited by Gary Scharnhorst and Denise D. Knight. — 1st ed.
      p. cm.
  Includes bibliographical references.
  ISBN 978-0-8156-3295-5 (cloth : alk. paper)
  I. Scharnhorst, Gary.   II. Knight, Denise D., 1954–   III. Title.
  PS1744.G57I6 2012
  811'.4—dc23                                                        2012013900

Manufactured in the United States of America

**GARY SCHARNHORST** is distinguished professor emeritus of English at the University of New Mexico in Albuquerque. He has published biographies on Horatio Alger, Jr., Bret Harte, Kate Field, and Charlotte Perkins Gilman.

**DENISE D. KNIGHT** is distinguished teaching professor of English at the State University of New York at Cortland. She is the author of a study examining Gilman's short fiction and the editor of Gilman's diaries, fiction, and later poetry.

# CONTENTS

## WOMAN

## THE MARCH

# Acknowledgments

WE WISH TO EXPRESS our sincere thanks to the following individuals and institutions for their kind assistance during the production of this volume. The staff at the Arthur and Elizabeth Schlesinger Library, Radcliffe Institute, and particularly Ellen M. Shea, Head of Public Services, deserves thanks for providing always-cheerful assistance with questions and permissions. Also deserving our thanks are Walter and Linda Chamberlin, for allowing us to use the photograph of Gilman that appears on the dust jacket. We also appreciate the meticulous reading of our manuscript by the two external reviewers who provided sound suggestions for revision. We are grateful to several people at Syracuse University Press: Lisa Kuebris, Marketing Coordinator, has been most helpful; Marcia Hough, Editorial Assistant, kept the project on schedule; and Victoria Lane, Senior Designer, did a fabulous job in creating the cover of the volume. We thank Michele T. Callaghan, our copy editor at Syracuse University Press, for providing guidance through the various stages of production. Finally, we extend thanks to Annelise Finegan and Jennika Baines, acquisitions editors at Syracuse University Press, for their ongoing and enthusiastic support of this project.

# A NOTE ON THE TEXT

THIS VOLUME reprints 261 of Gilman's poems, including 149 verses that appeared in the third American (or final) edition of *In This Our World,* as well as 112 vagrant verses that were produced throughout Gilman's career. Our purpose has been to make available to scholars, researchers, and students a comprehensive edition of the Gilman's early poetry. In addition to reprinting the third edition of *In This Our World,* the miscellaneous poetry we have collected has been taken from the journals, books, newspapers, and other documents in which the works originally appeared.

Because the role of an editor is to be less interpretive than objective, we used a conservative editorial method: our purpose has been to preserve the original appearance of the verses rather than to "improve" them through editorial emendations, while still providing as background an appropriate amount of historical and biographical contextualization. Throughout this project, textual and historical accuracy has been an overriding concern. Therefore, Gilman's own spelling, capitalization, punctuation, underlinings, indentations, and abbreviations have been preserved; the only exception we have made is to standardize the capitalization in some of the poem titles. We have also provided notes for places, people, events, words, or objects that might be unfamiliar to the contemporary reader or that might benefit from clarification. We have preserved the order in which Gilman's poems appeared in the third edition of *In This Our World*; the other vagrant poems have been presented chronologically.

Interested readers should consult Denise D. Knight's edition of *The Later Poetry of Charlotte Perkins Gilman,* which reprints a total of 164 poems, and Gary Scharnhorst's *Charlotte Perkins Gilman: A Bibliography* (1985; reprinted 2003, pp. 39–55) for a list of the 179 poems in *The Forerunner* not collected elsewhere.

# INTRODUCTION

CHARLOTTE PERKINS GILMAN (1860–1935), the most prominent intellectual in the American woman's movement early in the twentieth century, began her writing career as a poet. Her first collection of verse, entitled *In This Our World*, was issued in three different editions between 1893 and 1898. While all of Gilman's later poems appear in her monthly magazine, *The Forerunner*, (1909–1916) or have been collected in Denise D. Knight's *The Later Poetry of Charlotte Perkins Gilman* (1996), complete and accurate versions of Gilman's early poems are largely inaccessible to modern students of her work. None of the first three editions of *In This Our World* have been reprinted, and dozens of poems Gilman published have never been collected at all. *In This Our World and Uncollected Poems* fills this critical gap in Gilman scholarship.

Charlotte Anna Perkins was raised in genteel poverty in Providence, Rhode Island. Her father, Frederic Beecher Perkins, a professional librarian, was the nephew of the Unitarian minister Henry Ward Beecher and the writer Harriet Beecher Stowe. Her mother, Mary Westcott Perkins, was also the descendant of a distinguished New England family. Her parents' marriage ended in separation and eventual divorce. Charlotte Perkins briefly attended the Rhode Island School of Design in 1878–1879 and while still living in Providence befriended Grace Ellery Channing, the granddaughter of William Ellery Channing, founder of the American Unitarian Church. Though she harbored grave doubts about her adaptability to marriage, she wed the artist Charles Walter Stetson in May 1884. But "something" went "wrong from the first," as she later allowed.[1] The "immutable submission" required of "dutiful house-wives bred rebellion in me."[2] She framed her predicament in the poem "In Duty Bound," published in the Boston *Woman's Journal*, four months before the wedding:

In duty bound, a life hemmed in
    Whichever way the spirit turns to look;
No chance of breaking out, except by sin;
      Not even room to shirk—
        Simply to live, and work.[3]

The marriage became even more complicated with the birth of their daughter, Katharine, in March 1885. Gilman suffered a severe case of post-partum depression. To the duties of wife were added those of mother, and Gilman collapsed under the weight. Her self-reproach was unequivocal: "You were called to serve humanity," she wrote in her memoir, "and you cannot serve yourself. No good as a wife, no good as a mother, no good for anything. And you did it to yourself!"[4] She dramatized her plight in the third part of her poem "The Answer," printed in the *Woman's Journal* in early October 1886:

A maid was asked in marriage. Wise as fair,
She gave her answer with deep thought and prayer,

Expecting, in the holy name of wife,
Great work, great pain, and greater joy, in life.

She found such work as brainless slaves might do,
By day and night, long labor, never through;

Such pain—no language can her pain reveal;
It had no limit but her power to feel;

Such joy—life left in her sad soul's employ
Neither the hope nor memory of joy.[5]

In the spring of 1887 Charlotte Stetson traveled to Philadelphia to be treated for neurasthenia by the nerve specialist S. Weir Mitchell, renowned for his "rest cure" for women. She was "put to bed and kept there" for weeks, an experience on which she later based her now-famous story "The Yellow Wall-Paper." The regimen did not work. At the nadir of her illness, as she recalled, "I made a rag baby, hung it on a doorknob and played with it. I would crawl into remote closets and under beds—to hide from the grinding pressure of that profound distress."[6] Finally, in the fall of 1887, Charlotte and Walter Stetson agreed to separate and later to divorce.

Gilman eked out a living in California for most of the next eight years and tried to provide for her daughter, Katharine. Her divorce was finalized in April 1894, and the following month she sent Katharine across the continent to live with Stetson and his new wife, her longtime friend Grace Ellery Channing. She ever after referred to Grace as her "co-mother," a "second mother" to her daughter "fully as good as the first, better in some ways perhaps."[7] Predictably, she was soon condemned as an "unnatural mother." From her perspective, however, she had borne the brunt of sacrifice: "No one suffered" from the arrangement "but myself."[8] She also justified her decision in the poem "The Duty Farthest," published in *The Impress* in November 1894:

> Finding myself unfit to serve my own,
> I left them, sadly, and went forth alone
> Unto the world where all things wait to do—
> The harvest ripe—the laborers but few.[9]

Her decision to relinquish custody of her daughter was a bold bid to escape, for better or worse, the drudgery of kitchen and laundry and to launch a wider public career.

In the spring of 1894 Gilman moved to San Francisco to find new work. She was serving at the time as the president of the Pacific Coast Women's Press Association and editor of its eight-page monthly magazine, *The Impress*. In May 1894, the same month Katharine traveled east to her father and his new wife, Gilman unveiled a plan to assume ownership of the paper and to expand it to a sixteen-page weekly. She kept the paper afloat for several months, writing much of its contents, including many poems, before it failed in February 1895 for want of advertisers and subscribers. "This fiasco," Gilman later reflected, "showed me my standing in that city."[10] Rocked by the scandal that erupted after her divorce, Gilman borrowed money, pulled up stakes, and left for the East that summer to launch her career as a full-time, itinerant lecturer.

Gilman's bid to become a professional writer began upon her arrival in Pasadena, California, after her separation from Stetson. "Poetry was always a delight to me,"[11] she reminisced in her autobiography. She learned "miles of it"[12] by heart. Few of her early verses, however, had reached print, only "two or three bits" before her marriage and "a half-dozen or so" over the next several years. But Gilman had resolved to earn her living as a poet, at least in part, and in her "first year of freedom" in California she published twenty-three poems.[13] She drifted into the orbit of social progressives on the West Coast and soon championed the causes of socialism, the organization of labor, the abolition of sex slavery, suffrage, the professionalization of child care, and other reforms in her poetry and speeches. She burst on the national scene with her poem "Similar Cases," printed in the April 1890 issue of the

*Nationalist*, the monthly magazine of a Christian socialist movement inspired by Edward Bellamy's utopian novel *Looking Backward* and headquartered in Boston. William D. Howells, the so-called dean of American letters, wrote her that he had read the poem "many times with unfailing joy. . . . We have nothing since [James Russell Lowell's] Biglow Papers half so good for a good cause."[14] Her great-uncle Edward Everett Hale, famous for his story "The Man without a Country," congratulated her, too. The poem "is perfect," he wrote. "If I told you all I say of it and all that other people say I should turn your head. The idea was an inspiration." He proclaimed the poem "a great campaign document,"[15] while Gertrude Atherton averred that the humor of the poem "is so sharp and the satire so keen that any member of that sex which claims humor as its special prerogative would be glad to have written it."[16] Even Ambrose Bierce, a fierce critic of feminism, allowed that "Similar Cases" was a "delightful satire upon those of us who have not the happiness to think that the progress of humanity toward the light is subject to sudden and lasting acceleration."[17] Gilman ended her diary for 1890 by remarking that her "whole literary reputation dates . . . mainly from 'Similar Cases.'"[18]

The poem anchored a thin collection of seventy-three verses by Gilman issued under the title *In This Our World* by the Oakland printers McCombs and Vaughn in December 1893. It sold for a quarter mostly on consignment in bookstores and to friends and, as the poet later recounted, it "brought small returns in cash but much in reputation."[19] It was favorably reviewed in the *San Francisco Star* and the *Overland Monthly*, and Gilman noted in her diary six weeks after its appearance that her "little book is going off splendidly. . . . Splendid reviews of it, appreciative personal letters, orders from individuals, telegram for fifty copies from *Woman's Journal*; general enthusiasm. I must have a new edition."[20] Two more editions of *In This Our World* appeared over the next five years, each of them with unique contents. A London publisher, T. Fisher Unwin, issued a British edition with 80 poems, and a small San Francisco press brought out a second American edition with 122 poems, both in 1895; Small, Maynard and Co. of Boston published a third and final American edition with 149 poems in 1898. This edition was reprinted in London by G. P. Putnam's Sons in 1899, and Small, Maynard issued additional reprintings of it in 1908, 1913, and 1914.

Put another way, Gilman earned a reputation as a gifted, versatile, and prolific poet long before the publication of her sociological treatise *Women and Economics: A Study of the Economic Relation between Men and Women as a Factor in Social Evolution* (1898). Howells reviewed both the second and third American editions, the former in *Harper's Weekly* and the latter in the *North American Review*. The "implications of her satire are for social reform of a very radical kind," he noted before joking, "I am afraid that the acceptance of [her] satire is mostly confined to fanatics, philanthropists and other Dangerous Persons."[21] As late as 1911, Howells wrote Gilman that he had reread "Similar Cases" and found that his original enthusiasm for it was "unabated. . . . When the gods really wake up and begin to behave justly you will have no cause to complain."[22] Between 1890 and 1900 Gilman contributed poems regularly to such progressive papers as the Boston *Woman's Journal*, the Boston *Nationalist* and *New Nation*, *Kate Field's Washington*, the *Woman's Tribune*, the Chicago *Social Democrat*, the *Appeal to Reason*, and the *American Fabian*. In her marriage to George Houghton Gilman in 1900, she found a gentle and supportive partner. In 1904 she contributed a poem per week to the *Woman's Journal*. To her contemporaries she was not only a social theorist but also a literary artist. Bellamy wrote from Boston to tell her that the poem "The Survival of the Fittest" had "quite made your fame hereabouts!"[23] Upton Sinclair declared her "America's most brilliant woman poet and critic" and even mentioned her by name in his novel *The Jungle*;[24] Floyd Dell called her "first of all, a poet," the author of "the best satirical verses of modern times";[25] George Bernard Shaw quoted her poems in his letters;[26] the sociologist Lester Ward cited them in his essays;[27] and Woodrow Wilson recited them aloud.[28] When she read her poem "Mother to Child" at the Women's Suffrage Convention in Washington, D.C., in January 1896, it was received "with great applause," and the *Woman's Journal* reported that "[t]hose of us who have for years admired [her] remarkable bright poems were delighted to meet her."[29]

Her purpose in her poetry, as in all her published writings, was unapologetically didactic. She told an interviewer in 1896 that "I don't call [*In This Our World*] a book of poems. I call it a tool box. It was written to drive nails with."[30] Her emphasis on moral instruction rather than on felicity of style and phrase often frustrated even her sympathetic readers. As Walter Stetson confessed in his diary, "I wish she'd strive more for beauty in poetry than for didactics, for when she does let herself forget to preach she writes very very tender & lovely things."[31] Early in her career, Gilman was an accomplished technician, her verse composed according to the rules in regular meter and rhyme. She certainly adopted a variety of traditional models, particularly sonnets ("Heaven," "Pioneers"), rondeaux ("Where Memory Sleeps"), sestinas ("Homes"), triolets ("A Glimpse of New Orleans"), pantuns ("My Lady's Hat"), ballads ("Ballad of the Summer Sun"), fourteeners ("Self-Conceit"), chants royale ("In Honor") as well as odes, hymns, anthems, allegories, and parables. Her typical stanza-form in these early poems was borrowed from New England hymnody, quatrains of iambic tetrameter or pentameter, rhyming even-numbered lines; and her literary allusions were chiefly drawn from the classics or the Bible. She was also familiar with the poetry of Emily Dickinson soon after it reached print; among her papers is a transcription of Dickinson's "The Book of Martyrs," as Mabel Loomis Todd and Thomas Wentworth Higginson entitled it in *The Poems of Emily Dickinson* (1890).[32]

Gilman's introduction to the poetry of Walt Whitman, dating back to the days of her courtship in 1883, eventually helped to liberate her style, and she experimented with free verse for the rest of her life. That is, Gilman was indebted to Whitman for the increasingly irregular scansion and informal tone of her verse. As early as February 1891 she hailed Whitman as "America's greatest poet";[33] she carried with her a copy of *Leaves of Grass*, which her husband had forbid her from reading, during a two-year lecture tour in the late 1890s;[34] and as late as 1933, two years before her death, she still regarded Whitman as one of the two greatest Americans who ever lived.[35] In his review of *In This Our World* in 1898, Horace Traubel, chief of the Whitmaniacs, cautioned her audience not to think of her as a conventional poet:

> Read Birth, an opening door. Read The Lion Path, and courage will come easier to you. Read Heroism, and you will spiral your way to the summit of moral intuition. Read Part of the Battle and tighten your armor. Read The Modern Skeleton and partake of no more feasts till all may be fed. Read Wings. If you are a minor poet you will not wonder more why your poetry is minor. Here is a touch light as The Skylark's. Read Among the Gods. You will never again dare to accuse her of want of phrase, though her phrase is not cited in handbooks on versification. Read Motherhood, read Mother to Child. Woman never wrote so to woman before—never in such quick demand or passionate service. Then read all the poems in the final section, The March, especially The Wolf at the Door, and Hardly a Pleasure, the last powerfully dramatic in its contrasts. If you can maintain any prejudice against [the poet's] art after you have done as much as this I should be more than astonished. You have met a woman with no indecent reticences who sings because singing becomes her sentiment. Forgive yourself possible prejudices and hereafter talk less about rules of art and a little more about its substance.[36]

Much as Whitman grew and pruned *Leaves of Grass* through its nine editions, Gilman reshaped the various incarnations of *In This Our World*, usually adding poems, sometimes deleting them, always adjusting their order. For example, her poems "Ideas. (After Emerson)." and "The Teacher" appear only in the British edition. "If a Man May Not Eat Neither Can He

Work" originally appears in the British edition, is omitted from the second American edition, but is reprinted in the third American edition. Her poem "Birth" does not appear in either the first American or the British editions, appears more than three quarters of the way through the second American edition, and is the opening poem in the third American edition. This poem also resonates with Whitmanesque overtones, as in its opening stanza:

> Lord, I am born!
> I have built me a body
> Whose ways are all open
> Whose currents run free
> From the life that is thine
> Flowing ever within me,
> To the life that is mine
> Flowing outward through me.

Like Whitman, Gilman here celebrates the transcendent nature of the Self. Gone are the inhibitions and fears of earlier years: the apprehension and scars of the breakdown she suffered at the age of twenty-six.[37]

In selecting and arranging her poems for publication in the various editions of *In This Our World*, Gilman was sensitive to such formal matters as sequence. The final edition, like the restructuring of Gaul in Caesar's *Commentaries*, was divided into three parts: "The World" (mostly nature and humorous poems, carols, and prayers), "The Woman" (feminist poems), and "The March" (political poems). Gilman's best nature poems were about California (e.g., "From Russian Hill," "California Car Windows") because, as she allowed in her autobiography, "California always makes me sing."[38] The humorous poems (e.g., "Step Faster, Please," "The Pig and the Pearl") reveal her sense of humor in stark contrast to her polemical satires. The feminist poems in "The Woman," as Catherine J. Golden notes, "subvert patriarchal ideologies, challenge female subjugation, and argue for equal rights." In such lyrics as "Females" and "Wedded Bliss," Golden adds, Gilman "indicts economically dependent wives who serve the home and rear their children incompetently; she marshals efforts in the service of social change for women."[39] The poems in "The March" were calls to action, admonitions to help farmers ("Free Land is Not Enough"), aid the poor ("If a Man May Not Eat Neither Can He Work"), reform prisons ("How Many Poor!"), and organize workers ("His Own Labor," "To Labor"). Gilman's political instincts were populist but not radically leftist; she was a parlor socialist and a utopian, not a revolutionary. At the risk of stretching a point, in her poem "Nationalism" she anticipated by nearly fifty years the notion of

"Manself" John Steinbeck espoused in chapter 14 of *The Grapes of Wrath*: "We serve the nation, serving still ourselves— / Nay, not ourselves—ourself! We are but parts, / The unit is the state,—America!" She preferred the term "humanist" to "feminist" because she sought to improve the entire race, not a single sex.[40]

Her verses were not always inspired by the Muse. Like many young poets, Gilman sometimes resorted to sentimentality, the trite and clichéd (e.g., "immortal loveliness," "It is good to be alive when the trees shine green"). She tended to overuse exclamation points and too often punctuated her verse with archaicisms (e.g., "Elfsoon he died," "Why weepest thou so sore?"). She occasionally indulged in textbook examples of the pathetic fallacy (e.g., "Baby love came prancing by," "I ran against a Prejudice"). Her rhymes were sometimes inelegant, as in "Powell Street" where she rhymed "façade" and "made." Then again, such apparent clumsiness may be attributed to Gilman's New England accent. Dickinson, after all, once rhymed "Judea" and "too near."[41]

Still, to dismiss or denigrate these poems would be akin to ignoring Herman Melville's or Thomas Hardy's verse. Though best known today for her fiction and essays as Melville and Hardy were for their novels, Gilman was not a mere poet by avocation any more than were they. Her poems comprise a central part of her oeuvre, and they register dramatically the crises in her life and the cultural movements that shaped the literary landscape of her time. They deserve to be resurrected from the footnote and read, studied, and enjoyed again.

Gary Scharnhorst, University of New Mexico<br>Denise D. Knight, State University of New York, Cortland

# In This Our World
### (third edition, 1898)

## ❧ THE WORLD ❧

## Birth

Lord, I am born!
I have built me a body
Whose ways are all open,
Whose currents run free,
From the life that is thine
Flowing ever within me,
To the life that is mine
Flowing outward through me.

I am clothed, and my raiment
Fits smooth to the spirit,
The soul moves unhindered,
The body is free;
And the thought that my body
Falls short of expressing
In texture and color
Unfoldeth on me.

I am housed, O my Father!
My body is sheltered,
My spirit has room
'Twixt the whole world and me,
I am guarded with beauty and strength,
And within it
Is room for still union,
And birth floweth free.

And the union and birth
Of the house, ever growing,
Have built me a city—
Have born me a state—
Where I live manifold,
Many-voiced, many-hearted,
Never dead, never weary,
And oh! never parted!
The life of The Human,
So subtle—so great!

Lord, I am born!
From inmost to outmost
The ways are all open,
The currents run free,
From thy voice in my soul
To my joy in the people—
I thank thee, O God,
For this body thou gavest,
Which enfoldeth the earth—
Is enfolded by thee!

## Nature's Answer

### I.
A man would build a house, and found a place
As fair as any on the earth's fair face:

Soft hills, dark woods, smooth meadows richly green,
And cool tree-shaded lakes the hills between.

He built his house within this pleasant land,
A stately white-porched house, long years to stand;

But, rising from his paradise so fair,
Came fever in the night and killed him there.

"O lovely land!" he cried, "how could I know
That death was lurking under this fair show?"

And answered Nature, merciful and stern,
"I teach by killing; let the others learn!"

### II.
A man would do great work, good work and true;
He gave all things he had, all things he knew;

He worked for all the world; his one desire
To make the people happier, better, higher;

Used his best wisdom, used his utmost strength;
And, dying in the struggle, found at length,

The giant evils he had found the same,
And that the world he loved scarce knew his name.

"Has all my work been wrong? I meant so well!
I loved so much!" he cried. "How could I tell?"

And answered Nature, merciful and stern,
"I teach by killing; let the others learn."

### III.
A maid was asked in marriage. Wise as fair,
She gave her answer with deep thought and prayer,

Expecting, in the holy name of wife,
Great work, great pain, and greater joy, in life.

She found such work as brainless slaves might do,
By day and night, long labor, never through;

Such pain—no language can her pain reveal;
It had no limit but her power to feel;

Such joy—lift left in her sad soul's employ
Neither the hope nor memory of joy.

Helpless, she died, with one despairing cry,—
"I thought it good; how could I tell the lie?"

And answered Nature, merciful and stern,
"I teach by killing; let the others learn."

## The Commonplace

Life is so commonplace! Too fair
Were those young visions of the poet and seer.
Nothing exciting ever happens here.
Just eat and drink, and dress and chat;
Life is so tedious, slow, and flat,
And every day alike in everywhere!

Birth comes. Birth—
The breathing re-creation of the earth!
All earth, all sky, all God, life's deep sweet whole,
Newborn again to each new soul!
"Oh, are you? What a shame! Too bad, my dear!
How well you stand it, too! It's very queer
The dreadful trials women have to carry;
But you can't always help it when you marry.
Oh, what a sweet layette![1] What lovely socks!
What an exquisite puff and powder box!
Who is your doctor? Yes, his skill's immense—
But it's a dreadful danger and expense!"

Love comes. Love—
And the world widens at the touch thereof;
Deepens and lightens till the answer true
To all life's questions seems to glimmer through.
"Engaged? I knew it must be! What a ring!
Worth how much? Well, you are a lucky thing!
But how was Jack disposed of?" "Jack? Oh, he
Was just as glad as I was to be free.
You might as well ask after George and Joe
And all the fellows that I used to know!
I don't inquire for his past Kate and Carry—
Every one's pleased. It's time, you know, to marry."

Life comes. Life—
Bearing within it wisdom, work, and strife.
To do, to strive, to know, and, with the knowing,
To find life's widest purpose in our growing.
"How are you, Jim? Pleasant weather to-day!
How's business?" "Well, it doesn't come my way."
"Good morning, Mrs. Smith! I hope you're well!
Tell me the news!" "The news? There's none to tell.

The cook has left; the baby's got a tooth;
John has gone fishing to renew his youth.
House-cleaning's due—or else we'll have to move!
How sweet you are in that! Good-bye, my love!"

Death comes. Death—
Love cries to love, and no man answereth.
Death the beginning, Death the endless end,
Life's proof and first condition, Birth's best friend.
"Yes, it's a dreadful loss! No coming back!
Never again! How do I look in black?
And then he suffered so! Oh, yes, we all
Are well provided for. You're kind to call,
And Mrs. Green has lost her baby too!
Dear me! How sad! And yet what could they do?
With such a hard time as they have, you know,—
No doubt 'twas better for the child to go!"

Life is so dreary commonplace. We bear
One dull yoke, in the country or the town.
We're born, grow up, marry, and settle down.
I used to think—but then a man must live!
The Fates dole out the weary years they give,
And every day alike in everywhere.


## Homes—A Sestina

We are the smiling comfortable homes
With happy families enthroned therein,
Where baby souls are brought to meet the world,
Where women end their duties and desires,
For which men labor as the goal of life,
That people worship now instead of God.

Do we not teach the child to worship God?—
Whose soul's young range is bounded by the homes
Of those he loves, and where he learns that life
Is all constrained to serve the wants therein,
Domestic needs and personal desires,—
These are the early limits of his world.

And are we not the woman's perfect world,
Prescribed by nature and ordained of God,
Beyond which she can have no right desires,
No need for service other than in homes?
For doth she not bring up her young therein?
And is not rearing young the end of life?

And man? What other need hath he in life
Than to go forth and labor in the world,

And struggle sore with other men therein?
Not to serve other men, nor yet his God,
But to maintain these comfortable homes,—
The end of all a normal man's desires.

Shall not the soul's most measureless desires
Learn that the very flower and fruit of life
Lies all attained in comfortable homes,
With which life's purpose is to dot the world
And consummate the utmost will of God,
By sitting down to eat and drink therein.

Yea, in the processes that work therein—
Fulfilment of our natural desires—
Surely man finds the proof that mighty God
For to maintain and reproduce his life
Created him and set him in the world;
And this high end is best attained in homes.

Are we not homes? And is not all therein?
Wring dry the world to meet our wide desires!
We crown all life! We are the aim of God!


## A Common Inference

A night: mysterious, tender, quiet, deep;
Thrilling with insect voices; thick with stars;
No cloud between the dewdrops and red Mars;
The small earth whirling softly on her way,
The moonbeams and the waterfalls at play;
A million million worlds that move in peace,
    A million mighty laws that never cease;
And one small ant-heap, hidden by small weeds,
Rich with eggs, slaves and store of millet seeds.
    They sleep beneath the sod
        And trust in God.

A day: all glorious, royal, blazing bright;
Heavy with flowers; full of life and light;
Great fields of corn and sunshine; courteous trees;
Snow-sainted mountains; earth-embracing seas;
Wide golden deserts; slender silver streams;
Clear rainbows where the tossing fountain gleams;
And everywhere, in happiness and peace,
A million forms of life that never cease;
And one small ant-heap, crushed by passing tread,
Hath scarce enough alive to mourn the dead!
    They shriek beneath the sod,
        "There is no God!"

## The Rock and the Sea

The Rock.
I am the Rock, presumptuous Sea!
I am set to encounter thee.
Angry and loud or gentle and still,
I am set here to limit thy power, and I will!
    I am the Rock!

I am the Rock. From age to age
I scorn thy fury and dare thy rage.
Scarred by frost and worn by time,
Brown with weed and green with slime,
Thou may'st drench and defile me and spit in my face,
But while I am here thou keep'st thy place!
    I am the Rock!

I am the Rock, beguiling Sea!
I know thou art fair as fair can be,
With golden glitter and silver sheen,
And bosom of blue and garments of green.
Thou may'st pat my cheek with baby hands,
And lap my feet in diamond sands,
And play before me as children play;
But plead as thou wilt, I bar the way!
    I am the Rock!

I am the Rock. Black midnight falls;
The terrible breakers rise like walls;
With curling lips and gleaming teeth
They plunge and tear at my bones beneath.
Year after year they grind and beat
In storms of thunder and storms of sleet,—
Grind and beat and wrestle and tear,
But the rock they beat on is always there!
    I am the Rock!

The Sea.
I am the Sea. I hold the land
As one holds an apple in his hand,
Hold it fast with sleepless eyes,
Watching the continents sink and rise.
Out of my bosom the mountains grow,
Back to its depths they crumble slow;
The earth is a helpless child to me.
    I am the Sea!

I am the Sea. When I draw back
Blossom and verdure follow my track,
And the land I leave grows proud and fair,
For the wonderful race of man is there;

And the winds of heaven wail and cry
While the nations rise and reign and die,
Living and dying in folly and pain,
While the laws of the universe thunder in vain.
What is the folly of man to me?
    I am the Sea.

I am the Sea. The earth I sway;
Granite to me is potter's clay;
Under the touch of my careless waves
It rises in turrets and sinks in caves;
The iron cliffs that edge the land
I grind to pebbles and sift to sand,
And beach-grass bloweth and children play
In what were the rock of yesterday.
It is but a moment of sport to me.
    I am the Sea!

I am the Sea. In my bosom deep
Wealth and Wonder and Beauty sleep;
Wealth and Wonder and Beauty rise
In changing splendor of sunset skies,
And comfort the earth with rains and snows
Till waves the harvest and laughs the rose.
Flower and forest and child of breath
With me have life—without me, death.
What if the ships go down in me?
    I am the Sea!

## The Lion Path

I dare not!
    Look! the road is very dark;
The trees stir softly and the bushes shake,
The long grass rustles, and the darkness moves
Here—there—beyond!
There's something crept across the road just now!
And you would have me go?
Go *there*, through that live darkness, hideous
With stir of crouching forms that wait to kill?
Ah, *look*! See there! and there! and there again!
Great yellow glassy eyes, close to the ground!
Look! Now the clouds are lighter I can see
The long slow lashing of the sinewy tails,
And the set quiver of strong jaws that wait!
Go there? Not I! Who dares to go who sees
So perfectly the lions in the path?

Comes one who dares.

Afraid at first, yet bound
On such high errand as no fear could stay.
Forth goes he with the lions in his path.
And then—?

He dared a death of agony,
Outnumbered battle with the king of beasts,
Long struggle in the horror of the night,
Dared and went forth to meet—O ye who fear!
Finding an empty road, and nothing there,—
A wide, bare, common road, with homely fields,
And fences, and the dusty roadside trees—
Some spitting kittens, maybe, in the grass.

## Reinforcements

Yes, we despair. Because the night is long,
And all arms weary with the endless fight
With blind, black forces of insulted law
Which we continually disobey,
And know not how to honor if we would.
How can we fight when every effort fails,
And the vast hydra[2] looms before us still
Headed as thickly as at dawn of day,
Fierce as when evening fell on us at war?
We are aweary, and no help appears;
No light, no knowledge, no sure way to kill
Our ancient enemy. Let us give o'er!
We do but fight with fate! Lay down your arms!
Retreat! Surrender! Better live as slaves
Then fight forever on a losing field!

Hold, yet faint-hearted! Ye are not alone!
Into your worn-out ranks of weary men
Come mighty reinforcements, even now!
Look where the dawn is kindling in the east,
Brave with the glory of the better day,—
A countless host, an endless host, all fresh,
With unstained banners and unsullied shields,
With shining swords that point to victory,
And great young hearts that know not how to fear,—
The Children come to save the weary world!

## Heroism

It takes great strength to train
To modern service your ancestral brain;
To lift the weight of the unnumbered years

Of dead men's habits, methods, and ideas;
To hold that back with one hand, and support
With the other the weak steps of a new thought.

It takes great strength to bring your life up square
With your accepted thought, and hold it there;
Resisting the inertia that drags back
From new attempts to the old habit's track.
It is so easy to drift back, to sink;
So hard to live abreast of what you think!

It takes great strength to live where you belong
When other people think that you are wrong;
People you love, and who love you, and whose
Approval is a pleasure you would choose.
To bear this pressure and succeed at length
In living your belief—well, it takes strength.

And courage too. But what does courage mean
Save strength to help you face a pain foreseen?
Courage to undertake this lifelong strain
Of setting yours against your grandsire's brain;
Dangerous risk of walking lone and free
Out of the easy paths that used to be,
And the fierce pain of hurting those we love
When love meets truth, and truth must ride above?

But the best courage man has ever shown
Is daring to cut loose and think alone.
Dark as the unlit chambers of clear space
Where light shines back from no reflecting face.
Our sun's wide glare, our heaven's shining blue,
We owe to fog and dust they fumble through;
And our rich wisdom that we treasure so
Shines from the thousand things that we don't know.
But to think new—it takes a courage grim
As led Columbus over the world's rim.[3]
To think it cost some courage. And to go—
Try it. It taxes every power you know.

It takes great love to stir a human heart
To live beyond the others and apart.
A love that is not shallow, is not small,
Is not for one, or two, but for them all.
Love that can wound love, for its higher need;
Love that can have love though the heart may bleed;
Love that can lose love; family, and friend;
Yet steadfastly live, loving, to the end.
A love that asks no answer, that can live
Moved by one burning, deathless force,—to give.

Love, strength, and courage. Courage, strength, and love,
The heroes of all time are built thereof.

## Fire with Fire

There are creeping flames in the near-by grass;
There are leaping flames afar;
And the wind's black breath
Is hot with death,
The worst of the deaths that are!

And north is fire and south is fire,
And east and west the same;
The sunlight chokes,
The whole earth smokes,
The only light is flame!

But what do I care for the girdle of death
With its wavering wall and spire!
I draw the ring
Where I am the king.
And fight the fire with fire!

My blaze is not as wide as the world,
Nor tall for the world to see;
But the flames I make
For life's sweet sake,
Are between the fire and me.

That fire would burn in wantonness
All things that life must use;
Some thing I lay
In the dragon's way
And burn because I choose.

The sky is black, the air is red,
The earth is a flaming sea;
But I'm shielded well
In the seething hell,
By the fire that comes from me.

There is nothing on earth a man need fear,
Nothing so dark or dire;
Though the world is wide,
You have more inside,
You can fight fire with fire!

## The Shield

Fight! said the Leader. Stand and fight!
   How dare you yield!

What is the pain of the bitter blows,
The ache and sting and the blood that flows,
    To a losing field!

Yea, said they, you may stand and fight;
    We needs must yield!
What is the danger and pain to you,
When every blow falls fair and true
    On your magic shield?

The magical cuirass[4] over your breast,
    Leather and steel,
Guarded like that, of course you dare
To meet the storm of battle there—
    But we can feel!

The Leader fell where he fought alone.
    See the lifeblood start
Where one more blow has pierced too far,
Through a bosom hardened with scar on scar, —
The only shield, the only bar,
    For that great heart!

## To the Preacher

    Preach about yesterday, Preacher!
      The time so far away:
When the hand of Deity smoke and slew,
And the heathen plagued the stiff-necked Jew;[5]
Or when the Man of Sorrows came,[6]
And blessed the people who cursed his name—
    Preach about yesterday, Preacher!
      Not about to-day!

    Preach about to-morrow, Preacher!
      Beyond this world's decay:
Of the sheepfold Paradise we priced
When we pinned our faith to Jesus Christ;
Of those hot depths that shall receive
The goats who would not so believe—
    Preach about to-morrow, Preacher,
      Not about to-day!

    Preach about the old sins, Preacher!
      And the old virtues, too:
You must not steal nor take man's life,
You must not covet your neighbor's wife,[7]
And woman must cling at every cost
To her one virtue, or she is lost—

Preach about the old sin, Preacher!
    Not about the new!

Preach about the other man, Preacher!
    The man we all can see!
The man of oaths, the man of strife,
The man who drinks and beats his wife,
Who helps his mates to fret and shirk
When all they need is to keep at work—
    Preach about the other man, Preacher!
    Not about me!

## A Type

I am too little, said the Wretch,
    For any one to see.
Among the million men who do
This thing that I am doing too,
    Why should they notice me?

My sin is common as to breathe;
    It rests on every back.
And surely I am not to blame
Where everybody does the same,—
    Am not a bit more black!

And so he took his willing share
    In a universal crime,
Thinking that no reproach could fall
On one who shared the fault of all,
    Who did it all the time.

Then Genius came, and showed the world
    What thing it was they did;
How their offence had reached the poles
With stench of slain unburied souls,
    And all men cowered and hid.

Then Genius took that one poor Wretch
    For now the time was ripe;
Stripped him of every shield and blind,
And nailed him up for all mankind
    To study—as a type!

## Compromise

It is well to fight and win—
    If that may be;
It is well to fight and die therein—
    For such go free;

It is ill to fight and find no grave
    But a prison-cell;
To keep alive, yet live a slave—
    Praise those who fell!

But worst of all are those who stand
    With arms laid by,
Bannerless, helpless, no command,
    No battle-cry.

They live to save unvalued breath,
    With lowered eyes;
In place of victory, or death,—
    A compromise!

## Part of the Battle

There is a moment when with splendid joy,
With flashing blade and roar of thundering guns
And colors waving wide where triumph stands,
The last redoubt is carried; we have won!
This is the battle! We have conquered now!

But the long hours of marching in the sun,
The longer hours of waiting in the dark,
Deadly dishonored work of hidden spy,
The dull details of commissariat,
Food, clothing, medicine, the hospital,
The way the transportation mules are fed,—
These are the battle too, and victory's price.

And we, in days when no attack is feared
And none is hoped,—no sudden courage called,—
Should strengthen our intrenchments quietly,
Review the forces, exercise the troops,
Feeling the while, not "When will battle come?"
But, "This is battle! We are conquering now!"

## Step Faster, Please

Of all most aggravating things,
    If you are hot in haste,
Is to have a man in front of you
    With half a day to waste.

There is this one thing that justifies
    The man in the foremost place:
The fact that he is the man in front,
    The leader of the race.

But, for Heaven's sake, if you are ahead,
>     Don't dawdle at your ease!
You set the pace for the man behind;
>     Step faster, please!

## A New Year's Reminder

Better have a tender conscience for the record of your house,
And your own share in the work which they have done,
>     Though your private conscience aches
>     With your personal mistakes,
And you don't amount to very much alone,

Than to be yourself as spotless as a baby one year old,
Your domestic habits wholly free from blame,
>     While the company you stand with
>     Is a thing to curse a land with,
And your public life is undiluted shame.

For the deeds men do together are what saves the world to-day
By our common public work we stand or fall—
>     And your fraction of the sin
>     Of the office you are in
Is the sin that's going to damn you, after all!

## Out of Place

Cell, poor little cell,
Distended with pain,
Torn with the pressure
Of currents of effort
Resisted in vain;
Feeling sweep by you
The stream of nutrition,
Unable to take;
Crushed flat and inactive,
While shudder across you
Great forces that wake;
Alone—while far voices
Across all the shouting
Call you to your own;
Held fast, fastened close,
Surrounded, enveloped,
How you starve there alone!
Cell, poor little cell,
Let the pain pass—don't hold it!
Let the effort pass through you!
Let go! And give way!

You will find your own place;
You will join your own people;
See the light of your day!

## Little Cell

Little Cell! Little Cell! with a heart as big as heaven,
Remember that you are but a part!
This great longing in your soul
Is the longing of the whole,
And your work is not done with your heart!

Don't imagine, Little Cell,
That the work you do so well
Is the only work the world needs to do!
You are wanted in your place
For the growing of the race,
But the growing does not all depend on you!

Little Cell! Little Cell! with a race's whole ambition,
Remember there are others growing, too!
You've been noble, you've been strong;
Rest a while and come along;
Let the world take a turn and carry you!

## The Child Speaks

Get back! Give me air! Give me freedom and room,
The warm earth and bright water, the crowding sweet bloom
Of the flowers, and the measureless, marvelous sky,—
All of these all the time, and a shelter close by
Where silence and beauty and peace are my own
     In a chamber alone.

Then bring me the others! "A child" is a crime;
It is "children" who grow through the beautiful time
Of their childhood up into the age you are in.
"A child" must needs suffer and sicken and sin,
The life of a child needs the life of its kind,
     O ye stupid and blind!

Then the best of your heart and the best of your brain!
The face of all beauty! The soul without stain!
Your noblest! Your wisest! With us is the place
To consecrate life to the good of the race!
That our childhood may pass with the best you can give,
     And our manhood so live!

The wisdom of years, the experience deep
That shall laugh with our waking and watch with our sleep,

The patience of age, the keen honor of youth,
To guide us in doing and teach us in truth,
With the garnered ripe fruit of the world at our feet,
  Both the bitter and sweet!

What is this that you offer? One man's narrow purse!
One woman's strained life, and a heart straining worse!
Confined as in prisons—held down as in caves—
The teaching of tyrants—the service of slaves—
The garments of falsehood and bondage—the weight
  Of your own evil state.

And what is this brought as atonement for these?
For our blind misdirection, our death and disease;
For the grief of our childhood, the loss and the wrong;
For the pain of our childhood, the agony strong;
For the shame and the sin and the sorrow thereof—
  Dare you say it is love?

Love? First give freedom,—the right of the brute!
The air with its sunshine, the earth with its fruit.
Love? First give wisdom,—intelligent care,
That shall help to bring out all the good that is there.
Love? First give justice! There's nothing above!
  And then you may love!


## To a Good Many

O blind and selfish! Helpless as the beast
Who sees no meaning in a soul released
And given flesh to grow in—to work through!
Think you that God has nothing else to do
Than babble endlessly the same set phrase?
Are life's great spreading, upward-reaching ways
Laid for the beasts to climb on till the top
Is reached in you, you think, and there you stop!
They were raised up, obedient to force
Which lifted them, unwitting of their course.
You have new power, new consciousness, new sight;
You can help God! You stand in the great light
Of seeing him at work. You can go on
And walk with him, and feel the glory won.
And here you sit, content to toil and strive
To keep your kind of animal alive!
Why, friends! God is not through!
The universe is not complete in you.
You're just as bound to follow out his plan
And sink yourself in ever-growing Man

As ever were the earliest, crudest eggs
To grow to vertebrates with arms and legs.
Society holds not its present height
Merely that you may bring a child to light;
But you and yours live only in the plan
That's working out a higher kind of man;
A higher kind of life, that shall let grow
New powers and nobler duties than you know.
Rise to the thought! Live in the widening race!
Help make the State more like God's dwelling-place!
New paths for life divine, as yet untrod,—
A social body for the soul of God.

## How Would You?

Half of our misery, half our pain,
Half the dark background of our self-reproach,
Is thought of how the world has sinned before.
We, being one, one with all life, we feel
The misdemeanors of uncounted time;
We suffer in the foolishness and sins
Of races just behind us,—burn with shame
At their gross ignorance and murderous deeds;
We suffer back of them in the long years
Of squalid struggling savagery of beasts,—
Beasts human and subhuman; back of them
In helpless creatures eaten, hunted, torn;
In submerged forests dying in the slime;
And even back of that in endless years
Of hot convulsions of dismembered lands,
And slow constricting centuries of cold.
So in our own lives, even to this day,
We carry in the chambers of the mind
The tale of errors, failures, and misdeeds
That we call sins, of all our early lives.
And the recurrent consciousness of this
We call remorse. The unrelenting gauge,
Now measuring past error,—this is shame.
And in our feverish overconsciousness,
A retroactive and preactive sense,—
Fired with our self-made theories of sin,—
We suffer, suffer, suffer—half alive,
And half with the dead scars of suffering.

Friends, how would you, perhaps, have made the world?
Would you have balanced the great forces so
Their interaction would have bred no shock?

No cosmic throes of newborn continents,
No eras of the earth-encircling rain,—
Uncounted scalding tears that fell and fell
On molten worlds that hotly dashed them back
In storms of fierce repudiated steam?
Would you have made earth's gems without the fire,
Without the water, and without the weight
Of crushing cubic miles of huddled rock?
Would you have made one kind of animal
To live on air and spare the tender grass,
And stop him, somehow, when he grew so thick
That even air fell short. Or would you have
All plants and animals, and make them change
By some metempsychosis[8] not called death?
For, having them, you have to have them change,
For growth is change, and life is growth; and change
Implies—in this world—what we miscall pain.

You, wiser, would have made mankind, no doubt,
Not slowly, awfully, from dying brutes
Up into living humanness at last,
But fresh as Adam in the Hebrew tale;
Only you would have left the serpent out,
And left him, naked, in the garden still.[9]
Or somehow, dodging this, have still contrived
That he should learn the whole curriculum
And never miss a lesson—never fail—
Be born, like Buddha,[10] all accomplished, wise.
Would you have chosen to begin life old,
Well-balanced, cautious, knowing where to step,
And so untortured by the memory
Of childhood's foolishness and youth's mistakes?
Or, born a child, to have experience
Come to you softly without chance of loss,
Recurring years each rolling to your hand
In blissful innocent unconsciousness?

O dreamers with a Heaven and a Hell
Standing at either end of your wild rush
Away from the large peace of knowing God,
Can you not see that all of it is good?
Good, with the postulate that this is life,—
And that is all we have to argue from.
Childhood means error, the mistakes that teach;
But only rod and threat and nurse's tale,
Makes childhood's errors bring us shame and sin.
The race's childhood grows by error too,
And we are not attained to manhood yet.

But grief and shame are only born of lies.
Once see the lovely law that needs mistakes,
And you are young forever. This is Life.

## A Man Must Live

A man must live. We justify
Low shift and trick to treason high,
    A little vote for a little gold
    To a whole senate bought and sold,
By that self-evident reply.

But is it so? Pray tell me why
Life at such cost you have to buy?
    In what religion were you told
        A man must live?

There are time when a man must die.
Imagine, for a battle-cry,
    From soldiers, with a sword to hold,—
    From soldiers, with the flag unrolled,—
This coward's whine, this liar's lie,—
        A man must live!

## In Duty Bound

In duty bound, a life hemmed in
        Whichever way the spirit turns to look;
No chance of breaking out, except by sin;
            Not even room to shirk—
            Simply to live, and work.

An obligation pre-imposed, unsought,
        Yet binding with the force of natural law;[11]
The pressure of antagonistic thought;
            Aching within, each hour,
            A sense of wasting power.

A house with roof so darkly low
        The heavy rafters shut the sunlight out;
One cannot stand erect without a blow;
            Until the soul inside
            Craves for a grave—more wide.

A consciousness that if this thing endure,
        The common joys of life will dull the pain;
The high ideals of the grand and pure
            Die, as of course they must,
            Of long disuse and rust.

That is the worst. It takes supernal strength
    To hold the attitude that brings the pain;
And they are few indeed but stoop at length
        To something less than best,
        To find, in stooping, rest.


## Desire

Lo, I desire! Sum of the age's growth—
Fruit of evolving eras—king of life—
I, holding in myself the outgrown past
In all its ever-rising forms—desire.
With the first grass-blade, I desire the sun;
With every bird that breathes, I love the air;
With fishes, joy in water; with my horse,
Exult in motion; with all living flesh,
Long for sweet food and warmth and mate and young;
With the whole rising tide of that which is,
Thirst for advancement,—crave and yearn for it!
Yea, I desire! Then the compelling will
Urges to action to attain desire.
What action? Which desire? Am I a plant,
Rooted and helpless, following the light
Without volition? Or am I a beast,
Led by desire into the hunter's snare?
Am I a savage, swayed by every wish,
Brutal and feeble, a ferocious child?
Stand back, Desire, and put your plea in words.
No wordless wailing for the summer moon,
No Gilpin race on some strong appetite,[12]
Stand here before the King, and make your plea
If Reason sees it just, you have your wish;
If not, your wish is vain, plead as you will.
The court is open, beggar! I am King!


## Why Not?

Why not look forward far as Plato looked
And see the beauty of our coming life,[13]
As he saw that which might be ours to-day?
If his soul, then, could rise so far beyond
The brutal average of that old time,
When icy peaks of art stood sheer and high
In fat black valleys where the helot[14] toiled;
If he, from that, could see so far ahead,
Could forecast days when Love and Justice both
Should watch the cradle of a healthy child,

And Wisdom walk with Beauty and pure Joy
In all the common ways of daily life,—
Then may not we, from great heights hardly won,
Bright hills of liberty, broad plains of peace,
And flower-sweet valleys of warm human love,
Still broken by the chasms of despair
Where Poverty and Ignorance and Sin
Pollute the air of all,—why not, from this
Look on as Plato looked, and see the day
When his Republic and our Heaven, joined,
Shall make life what God meant it?
    Ay, we do!

## Out of the Gate

Out of the glorious city gate
A great throng came.
A mighty throng that swelled and grew
Around a face that all men knew—
A man who bore a noted name—
Gathered to listen to his fate.

The Judge sat high. Unbroken black
Around, above, and at his back.
The people pressed for nearer place,
Longing, yet shamed, to watch that face;
And in a space before the throne
The prisoner stood, unbound, alone.
So thick they rose on every side,
There was no spot his face to hide.

Then came the Herald, crying clear,
That all the listening crowd should hear;
Crying aloud before the sun
What thing this fallen man had done.
He—who had held a ruler's place
Among them, by their choice and grace—
He—fallen lower than the dust—
Had sinned against his public trust!

The Herald ceased. The Poet arose,
The Poet, whose awful art now shows
To this poor heart, and heart of every one,
The horror of the thing that he had done.

"O Citizen! Dweller in this high place!
Son of the city! Sharer in its pride!
Born in the light of its fair face!
By it fed, sheltered, taught, and glorified!

Raised to pure manhood by thy city's care;
Made strong and beautiful and happy there;
Loving thy mother and thy father more
For the fair town which made them glad before;
Finding among its maidens thy sweet wife;
Owing to it thy power and place in life;
Raised by its people to the lofty stand
Where thou couldst execute their high command;
Trusted and honored, lifted over all,—
So honored and so trusted, didst thou fall!
Against the people—who gave thee the power—
Thou hast misused it in an evil hour!
Against the city where thou owest all—
Thy city, man, within whose guarding wall
Lie all our life's young glories—ay, the whole!
The home and cradle of the human soul!
Against thy city, beautiful and strong,
Thou, with the power it gave, hast done this wrong!"

Then rose the Judge. "Prisoner, thy case was tried
Fairly and fully in the courts inside.
Thy guilt was proven, and thou hast confessed,
And now the people's voice must do the rest.
I speak the sentence which the people give:
It is permitted thee to freely live,
Redeem thy sin by service to the state,
But nevermore within this city's gate!"

Back rolled the long procession, sad and slow,
Back where the city's thousand banners blow.
The solemn music rises glad and clear
When the great gates before them open near,
Rises in triumph, sinks to sweet repose,
When the great gates behind them swing and close.
Free stands the prisoner, with a heart of stone.
The city gate is shut. He is alone.

## The Modern Skeleton

As kings of old in riotous royal feasts,
Among the piled up roses and the wine,
Wild music and soft-footed dancing girls,
The pearls and gold and barbarous luxury,
Used to show also a white skeleton,—
To make life meeker in the sight of death,
To make joy sweeter by the thought thereof,—

So our new kings in their high banqueting,
With the electric luster unforeseen,

And unimagined costliness of flowers;
Rich wines of price and food as rare as gems,
And all the wondrous waste of artifice;
Midst high-bred elegance and jeweled ease
And beauty of rich raiment; they should set
High before all, a sickly pauper child,
To keep the rich in mind of poverty,—
The sure concomitant of their estate.

## The Lesson of Death—to S.T.D.

In memory of one whose breath
Blessed all with words wise, loving, brave;
Whose life was service, and whose death
Unites our hearts around her grave.

. . . . . . . .

Another blow has fallen, Lord—
    Was it from thee?
Is it indeed thy fiery sword
That cuts our hearts? We know thy word;
"Whom the Lord loves he chasteneth"[15]—
But also, in another breath,
This: "The wages of sin is death."[16]

How may we tell what pain is good,
    In mercy sent?
And what is evil through and through,
Sure consequence of what we do,
Sure product of thy broken laws,
Certain effect of given cause,
    Just punishment?

Not sin of those who suffer, Lord—
    To them no shame.
For father's sins our children die
With Justice sitting idly by;
The guilty thrive nor yet repent,
While sorrow strikes the innocent—
    Whom shall we blame?

'Tis not that one alone is dead,
    And these bereft.
For her, for them, we grieve indeed;
But there are other hearts that bleed!
All up and down the world so wide
We suffer, Lord, on every side,—
    We who are left.

See now, we bend our stricken hearts,
    Patient and still,

Knowing thy laws are wholly just,
Knowing thy love commands our trust,
Knowing that good is God alone,
That pain and sorrow are our own,
And seeking out of all our pain
To struggle up to God again—
    Teach us thy will!

When shall we learn by common joy
    Broad as the sun,
By common effort, common fear,
All common life that holds us near,
And this great bitter common pain
Coming again and yet again—
    That we are one?

Yea, one. We cannot sin apart,
    Suffer alone;
Nor keep our goodness to ourselves
Like precious things on hidden shelves.
Because we each live not our best,
Some one must suffer for the rest—
    For we are one!

Our pain is but the voice of wrong—
    Lord, help us hear!
Teach us to see the truth at last,
To mend our future from our past,
To know thy laws and find them friends,
Leading us safe to lovely ends,
    Thine own hand near.

Not one by doing right alone
    Can mend the way;
But we must all do right together,—
Love, help, and serve each other, whether
We joy or suffer. So at least
Shall needless pain and death be past,
And we, thy children living here,
Be worthy of our father dear!
    God speed the day!

. . . . . . . . .

Oh, help us, Father, from this loss
    To learn thy will!
So shall our lost one live again;
So shall her life not pass in vain;
So shall we show in better living—
In loving, helping, doing, giving—
    That she lives still!

## For Us

If we have not learned that God's in man,
    And man in God again;
That to love thy God is to love thy brother,
And to serve the Lord is to serve each other,—
    Then Christ was born in vain!

If we have not learned that one man's life
    In all men lives again;
That each man's battle, fought alone,
Is won or lost for every one,—
    Then Christ hath lived in vain!

If we have no learned that death's no break
    In life's unceasing chain;
That the work in one life well begun
In others is finished, by others is done,—
    Then Christ hath died in vain!

If we have not learned of immortal life,
    And a future free from pain;
The kingdom of God in the heart of man,
And the living world on Heaven's plan,—
    Then Christ arose in vain!


## Thanksgiving

Well is it for the land whose people, yearly,
    Turn to the Giver of all Good with praise,
Chanting glad hymns that thank him, loudly, clearly,
    Rejoicing in the beauty of his ways.

Great name that means all perfectness and power!
    We thank thee—not for mercy, nor release,
But for clear joy in sky and sea and flower,
    In thy pure justice, and thy blessed peace.

We live; behind us the dark past; before,
    A wide way full of light that thou dost give;
More light, more strength, more joy and ever more—
    O God of joy! we thank thee that we live!


## Christmas Hymn

Listen not to the word that would have you believe
That the voice of the age is a moan;
    That the red hand of wrong
    Is triumphant and strong,
And that wrong is triumphant alone;

There was never a time on the face of the earth
　　When love was so near its own

Do you think that the love which has died for the world
Has not lived for the world also?
　　Filling man with the fire
　　Of a boundless desire
To love all with a love that shall grow?
It was not for nothing the White Christ[17] was born
　　Two thousand years ago.

The power that gave birth to the Son of the King
All life doth move and thrill,
　　Every age as 'tis passed
　　Coming nearer at last
To the law of that wonderful will,—
As our God so loved the world that day,
　　Our God so loves it still.

The love that fed poverty, making it thrive,
Is learned a lovelier way.
　　We have seen that the poor
　　Need be with us no more,
And that sin may be driven away;
The love that has carried the martyrs to death
　　Is entering life to-day.

The spirit of Christ is awake and alive,
In the work of the world it is shown,
　　Crying loud, crying clear,
　　That the Kingdom is here,
And that all men are heirs to the throne!
There was never a time since the making of man
　　When live was so near its own!


## Christmas

Slow, slow and weak,
As first the tongue began to speak,
The hand to serve, the heart to feel,
Grew up among our mutual deeds,
Great flower out-topping all the weeds,
Sweet fruit that meets all human needs,
　　Our love—our common weal.

It spread so wide, so high,
We saw it broad against the sky,
Down shining where we trod;
It stormed our new-born consciousness,

Omnipotent to heal and bless,
Till we conceived—we could no less,
    It was the love of God!

Came there a man at length
Whose heart so swelled with the great strength
Of love that would have way,
That in his body he fulfilled
The utmost service had willed;
And the great steam, so help, so spilled,
    Pours on until to-day.

Still we look back to the grand dream,
Still stoop to drink at this wide stream,
Wider each year we live;
And on one yearly blessed day,
Seek not to earn and not to pay,
But to let love have its one way,—
    To quench our thirst *to give*!

Brothers, cease not to bless the name
Of him who loved through death and shame,
We cannot praise amiss;
But not in vain was sown the seed;
Look wide where thousands toil and bleed,
Where men meet death for common need—
    Hath no man loved but this?

Yea, all men love; we love to-day
Wide as the human race has sway,
Ever more deep, more dear;
No stream,—an everlasting sea,
Beating and throbbing to be free,
To give it forth there needs must be
    One Christmas all the year!

## The Living God

The Living God. The God that made the world
Made it, and stood aside to watch and wait,
Arranging a predestined plan
To save the erring soul of man—
Undying destiny—unswerving fate.
I see his hand in the path of life,
His law to doom and save,
His love divine in the hopes that shine
Beyond the sinner's grave,
His care that sendeth sun and rain,
His wisdom giving rest,

His price of sin that we may not win
The heaven of the blest.

> Not near enough! Not clear enough!
>     O God, come nearer still!
> I long for thee! Be strong for me!
>     Teach me to know thy will!

The Living God. The God that makes the world,
Makes it—is making it in all its worth;
His spirit speaking sure and slow
In the real universe we know,—
God living in the earth.
I feel his breath in the blowing wind,
His pulse in the swinging sea,
And the sunlit sod is the breast of God
Whose strength we feel and see.
His tenderness in the spring grass,
His beauty in the flowers,
His living love in the sun above,—
All here, and near, and ours!

> Not near enough! Not clear enough!
>     O God, come nearer still!
> I long for thee! Be strong for me!
>     Teach me to know thy will!

The Living God. The God that is the world.
The world? The world is man,—the work of man.
Then—dare I follow what I see?—
Then—by thy Glory—it must be
That we are in thy plan?
That strength divine in the work we do?
That love in our mothers' eyes?
That wisdom clear in our thinking here?
That power to help us rise?
God in the daily work we've done,
In the daily path we've trod?
Stand still, my heart, for I am a part—
I too—of the Living God!

> Ah, clear as light! As near! As bright!
>     O God! My God! My Own!
> Command thou me! I stand for thee!
>     And I do not stand alone!

## A Prayer

O God! I cannot ask thee to forgive;
    I have done wrong.

Thy law is just; thy law must live,—
Whoso doth wrong must suffer pain.
But help me to do right again,—
　　Again be strong.


## Give Way!

Shall we not open the human heart,
Swing the doors till the hinges start;
　　Stop our worrying doubt and din,
　　Hunting heaven and dodging sin?
There is no need to search so wide,
Open the door and stand aside—
　　Let God in!

Shall we not open the human heart
To loving labor in field and mart;
　　Working together for all about,
　　The glad, large labor that knows not doubt?
Can He be held in our narrow rim?
Do the work that is work for Him—
　　Let God out!

Shall we not open the human heart,
Never to close and stand apart?
　　God is a force to give way to!
　　God is a thing you have to do!
God can never be caught by prayer,
Hid in your heart and fastened there—
　　Let God through!


## Thanksgiving Hymn—for California

Our forefathers gave thanks to God,
　　In the land by the stormy sea,
For bread hard wrung from the iron sod
　　In cold and misery.
Though every day meant toil and strife,
　　In the land by the stormy sea,
They thanked their God for the gift of life—
　　How much the more should we!

Stern frost had they full many a day,
　　Strong ice on the stormy sea,
Long months of snow, gray clouds hung low,
　　And a cold wind endlessly;
Winter, and war with an alien race—
　　But they were alive and free!

And they thanked their God for his good grace—
    How much the more should we!

For we have a land all sunny with gold,—
    A land by the summer sea;
Gold in the earth for our hands to hold,
    Gold in blossom and tree;
Comfort, and plenty, and beauty, and peace,
    From the mountains down to the sea.
They thanked their God for a year's increase—
    How much the more should we!

## Christmas Carol—for Los Angeles

On the beautiful birthday of Jesus,
    While the nations praising stand,
He goeth from city to city,
    He walketh from land to land.

And the snow lies white and heavy,
    And the ice lies wide and wan,
But the love of the blessed Christmas
    Melts even the heart of man.

With love from the heart of Heaven,
    In the power of his Holy Name,
To the City of the Queen of the Angels
    The tender Christ-child came.

The land blushed red with roses,
    The land laughed glad with grain,
And the little hills smiled softly
    In the freshness after rain.

Land of the fig and olive!
    Land of the fruitful vine!
His heart grew soft within him,
    As he thought of Palestine,

Of the brooks with the banks of lilies,
    Of the little doves of clay,
And of how he sat with his mother
    At the end of a summer's day,

His head on his mother's bosom,
    His hand in his mother's hand,
Watching the golden sun go down
    Across the shadowy land,—

A moment's life with human kind;
    A moment,—nothing more;

Eternity lies broad behind,
　　Eternity before.

High on the Hills of Heaven,
　　Majestic, undefiled,
Forever and ever he lives, a God;
　　But once he lived, a Child!

And the child-heart leaps within him,
　　And the child-eyes softer grow,
When the land lies bright and sunny,
　　Like the land of long ago;

And the love of God is mingled
　　With the love of dear days gone,
When he comes to the city of his mother,
　　On the day her child was born!


## New Duty

Once to God we owed it all,—
　　God alone;
Bowing in eternal thrall,
Giving, sacrificing all,
　　Before the Throne.

Once we owed it to the King,—
　　Served the crown;
Life, and love, and everything,
In allegiance to the King,
　　Laying down.

Now we owe it to Mankind,—
　　To our Race;
Fullest fruit of soul and mind,
Heart and hand and all behind,
　　Now in place.

Loving-service, wide and free,
　　From the sod
Up in varying degree,
Through me and you—through you and me—
　　Up to God!


## Seeking

I went to look for Love among the roses, the roses,
The pretty winged boy with the arrow and the bow;[18]
　　In the fair and fragrant places,
　　　'Mid the Muses and the Graces,[19]
At the feet of Aphrodite,[20] with the roses all aglow.

Then I sought among the shrines where the rosy flames were leaping—
The rose and golden flames, never ceasing, never still—
>   For the boy so fair and slender,
>   The imperious, the tender,
With the whole world moving slowly to the music of his will

Sought, and found not for my seeking, till the sweet quest led me further,
And before me rose the temple, marble-based and gold above,
>   Where the long procession marches
>   'Neath the incense-clouded arches
In the world-compelling worship of the mighty God of Love.

Yea, I passed with bated breath to the holiest of holies,
And I lifted the great curtain from the Inmost,—the Most Fair,—
>   Eager for the joy of finding,
>   For the glory, beating, blinding,
Meeting but an empty darkness; darkness, silence—nothing there.

Where is Love? I cried in anguish, while the temple reeled and faded;
Where is Love?—for I must find him, I must know and understand!
>   Died the music and the laughter,
>   Flames and rose dying after,
And the curtain I was holding fell to ashes in my hand.


## Finding

Out of great darkness and wide wastes of silence,
>   Long loneliness, and slow untasted years,
>   Came a slow filling of the empty places,
>   A slow, sweet lighting of forgotten faces,
>       A smiling under tears.

A light of dawn that filled the brooding heaven,
>   A warmth that kindled all the earth and air,
>   A thrilling tender music, floating, stealing,
>   A fragrance of unnumbered flowers revealing
>       A sweetness new and fair.

After the loss of love where I had sought him,
>   After the anguish of the empty shrine,
>   Came a warm joy from all the hearts around me,
>   A feeling that some perfect strength had found me,
>       Touch of the hand divine.

I followed Love to his intensest centre,
>   And lost him utterly when fastened there;
>   I let him go and ceased my selfish seeking,
>   Turning my heart to all earth's voices speaking,
>       And found him everywhere.

Love like the rain that falls on just and unjust,
Love like the sunshine, measureless and free,
From each to all, from all to each, to live in;
And, in the world's glad love so gladly given,
Came heart's true love to me!

## Too Much

There are who die without love, never seeing
The clear eyes shining, the bright wings fleeing.
Lonely they die, and ahungered, in bitterness knowing
They have not had their share of the good there was going.

There are who have and lose love, these most blessed,
In joy unstained which they have once possessed,
Lost while still dear, still sweet, still met by glad affection,—
An endless happiness in recollection.

And some have Love's full cup as he doth give it—
Have it, and drink of it, and, ah,—out live it!
Full fed by Love's delights, o'erwearied, sated,
They die, not hungry—only suffocated.

## The Cup

And yet, saith he, ye need but sip;
    And who would die without a taste?
Just touch the goblet to the lip,
    The let the bright draught run to waste!

She set her lip to the beaker's brim—
    'Twas passing sweet! 'Twas passing mild!
She let her large eyes dwell on him,
    And sipped again, and smiled.

So sweet! So mild! She scarce can tell
    If she doth really drink or no;
Till the light doth fade and the shadows swell,
    And the goblet lieth low.

O cup of dreams! O cup of doubt!
    O cup of blinding joy and pain!
The taste that none would die without!
    The draught that all the world must drain!

## What Then?

Suppose you write your heart out till the world
    Sobs with one voice—what then?

Small agonies that round your heart-strings curled
    Strung out for choice, that men
May pick a phrase, each for his own pet pain,
    And thank the voice so come,
    They being dumb. What then?

You have no sympathy? O endless claim!
    No one that cares? What then?
Suppose you had—the whole world knew your name
    And your affairs, and men
Ached with your headache, dreamed your dreadful dreams,
    And, with your heart-break due,
    Their hearts broke too. What then?

You think that people do not understand?
    You suffer? Die? What then?
Unhappy child, look here, on either hand,
Look low or high,—all men
Suffer and die, and keep it to themselves!
    They die—they suffer sore—
    You suffer more? What then?


## Our Loneliness

There is no deeper grief than loneliness.
Our sharpest anguish at the death of friends
Is loneliness. Our agony of heart
When love has gone from us is loneliness.
The crying of a little child at night
In the big dark is crowding loneliness.
Slow death of woman on a Kansas farm;
The ache of those who think beyond their time;
Pain unassuaged of isolated lives,—
All this is loneliness.

Oh, we who are one body of one soul!
Great soul of man born into social form!
Should we not suffer at dismemberment?
A finger torn from brotherhood; an eye
Having no cause to see when set alone.
Our separation is the agony
Of uses unfulfilled—of thwarted law;
The forces of all nature throb and push,
Crying for their accustomed avenues;
And we, alone, have no excuse to be,—
No reason for our being. We are dead
Before we die, and know it in our hearts.

Even the narrowest union has some joy,
Transient and shallow, limited and weak;

And joy of union strengthens with its strength,
Deepens and widens as the union grows.
Hence the pure light of long-enduring love,
Lives blended slowly, softly, into one.
Hence civic pride, and glory in our states,
And the fierce thrill of patriotic fire
When millions feel as one!

When we shall learn
To live together fully; when each man
And woman works in conscious interchange
With all the world,—union as wide as man,—
No human soul can ever suffer more
The devastating grief of loneliness.


## The Keeper of the Light

A lighthouse keeper with a loving heart
    Toiled at his service in the lonely tower,
Keeping his giant lenses clear and bright,
And feeding with pure oil the precious light
    Whose power to save was as his own heart's power.

He loved his kind, and being set alone
    To help them by the means of his great light,
He poured his whole heart's service into it,
And sent his love down the long beams that lit
    The waste of broken water in the night.

He loved his kind, and joyed to see the ships
    Come out of nowhere into his bright field,
And glide by safely with their living men,
Past him and out into the dark again,
    To other hands their freight of joy to yield.

His work was noble and his work was done;
    He kept the ships in safety and was glad;
And yet, late coming with the light's supplies,
They found the love no longer in his eyes—
    The keeper of the light had fallen mad.


## Immortality

When I was grass, perhaps I may have wept
As every year the grass-blades paled and slept;
Or shrieked in anguish impotent, beneath
The smooth impartial cropping of great teeth—
I don't remember much what came to pass
    When I was grass.

When I was monkey, I'm afraid the trees
Weren't always havens of contented ease;
Things killed us, and we never could tell why;
No doubt we blamed the earth or sea or sky—
I have forgotten my rebellion's shape
    When I was ape.

Now I have reached the comfortable skin
This stage of living is enveloped in,
And hold the spirit of my mighty race
Self-conscious prisoner under one white face,—
I'm awfully afraid I'm going to die,
    Now I am I.

So I have planned a hypothetic life
To pay me somehow for my toil and strife.
Blessed or damned, I someway must contrive
That I eternally be kept alive!
In this an endless, boundless bliss I see,—
    Eternal me!

.  .  .  .  .  .  .  .

When I was man, no doubt I used to care
About the little things that happened there,
And fret to see the years keep going by,
And nations, families, and persons die.
I didn't much appreciate life's plan
When I was man.

## Waste

Doth any man consider what we waste
Here in God's garden? While the sea is full,
The sunlight smiles, and all the blessed earth
Offers her wealth to our intelligence.
We waste our food, enough for half the world,
In helpless luxury among the rich,
In helpless ignorance among the poor,
In spilling what we stop to quarrel for.
We waste our wealth in failing to produce,
In robbing of each other every day
In place of making things,—our human crown.
We waste our strength, in endless effort poured
Like water on the sand, still toiling on
To make a million things we do not want.
We waste our lives, those which should still lead on,
Each new one gaining on the age behind,
In doing what we all have done before.

We waste our love,—poured into the sky,
Across the ocean, into desert lands,
Sunk in one narrow circle next ourselves,—
While these, our brothers, suffer—are alone.
Ye may not pass the near to love the far;
Ye may not love the near and stop at that.
Love spreads through man, not over or around!
Yea, grievously we waste; and all the time
Humanity is waiting,—wanting sore.
Waste not, my brothers, and ye shall not want!

## Wings

A sense of wings—
    Soft downy wings and fair—
Great wings that whistle as they sweep
Along the still gulfs—empty, deep—
    Of thin blue air.

    Doves' wings that follow,
        Doves' wings that fold,
    Doves' wings that flutter down
        To nestle in your hold.

    Doves' wings that settle,
        Doves' wings that rest,
    Doves' wings that brood so warm
        Above the little nest.

    Larks' wings that rise and rise,
    Climbing the rosy skies—
        Fold and drop down
        To birdlings brown.

Light wings of wood-birds, that one scarce believes
        Moved in the leaves.

    The quick, shy flight
    Of wings that flee in fright—
    A start as swift as light—
    Only the shaken air
    To tell that wings were there.

Broad wings that beat for many days
Above the land wastes and the water ways;
    Beating steadily on and on,
        Through dark and cold,
        Through storms untold,
    Till the far sun and summer land is won.

And wings—
        Wings that unfold
With such wide sweep before your would-be hold—
Such glittering sweep of whiteness—sun on snow—
Such mighty plumes—strong-ribbed, strong-webbed—strong-knit to go
        From earth to heaven!
        Hear the air flow back
        In their wide track!
    Feel the sweet wind these wings displace
        Beat on your face!
See the great arc of light like rising rockets trail
        They leave in leaving—
        They avail—
        These wings—for flight!

## The Heart of the Water

O the ache in the heart of the water that lies
Underground in the desert, unopened, unknown,
While the seeds lie unbroken, the blossoms unblown,
And the traveller wanders—the traveller dies!

O the joy in the heart of the water that flows
From the well in the desert,—a desert no more,—
Bird-music and blossoms and harvest in store,
And the white shrine that showeth the traveler knows!

## The Ship

The sunlight is mine! And the sea!
    And the four wild winds that blow!
The winds of heaven that whistle free—
They are but slaves to carry me
        Wherever I choose to go!

Fire for a power inside!
    Air for a pathway free!
I traverse the earth in conquest wide;
The sea is my servant! The sea is my bride!
        And the elements wait on me!

. . . . . . . .

In dull green light, down-filtered sick and slow
Through miles of heavy water overhead,

With miles of heavy water yet below,
        A ship lies, dead.
Shapeless and broken, swayed from side to side,
The helpless driftwood of an unknown tide.

## Among the Gods

How close the air of valleys, and how close
The teeming little life that harbors there!
For me, I will climb mountains. Up and up,
Higher and higher, till I pant for breath
In that thin clearness. Still? There is no sound
Nor memory of sound upon these heights.
Ah! the great sunlight! The caressing sky,
The beauty, and the stillness, and the peace!
I see my pathway clear for miles below;
See where I fell, and set a friendly sign
To warn some other of the danger there.
The green small world is wide below me spread.
The great small world! Some things look large and fair
Which, in their midst, I could not even see;
And some look small which used to terrify.
Blessed these heights of freedom, wisdom, rest!
I will go higher yet.

      A sea of cloud
Rolls soundless waves between me and the world,
This is the zone of everlasting snows,
And the sweet silence of the hills below
Is sing and laughter to the silence here.
Great fields, huge peaks, long awful slopes of snow.
Alone, triumphant, man above the world,
I stand among these white eternities.

      Sheer at my feet
Sink the unsounded, cloud-encumbered gulfs;
And shifting mists now veil and now reveal
The unknown fastnesses above me yet.
I am alone—above all life—sole king
Of these white wastes. How pitiful and small
Becomes the outgrown world! I reign supreme,
And in this utter stillness and wide peace
Look calmly down upon the universe.

Surely that crest has changed! That pile of cloud
That covers half the sky, waves like a robe!
      That large and gentle wind
Is like the passing of a presence here!
See how yon massive mist-enshrouded peak
Is like the shape of an unmeasured foot,—
The figure with the stars!
Ah! what is this? It moves, lifts, bends, is gone!

With what a shocking sense of littleness—
A reeling universe that changes place,

And falls to new relation over me—
I feel the unseen presence of the gods!

## Songs

I

    O world of green, all shining, shifting!
    O world of blue, all living, lifting!
O world where glassy waters smoothly roll!
    Fair earth, and heaven free,
    Ye are but part of me—
    Ye are my soul!

    O woman nature, shining, shifting!
    O woman creature, living, lifting!
Come soft and still to one who waits thee here!
    Fair soul, both mine and free,
    Ye who are part of me,
        Appear! Appear!

II

How could I choose but weep?
The poor bird lay asleep;
For lack of food, for lack of breath,
For lack of life he came to death—
How could I choose but weep?

How could I choose but smile?
There was no lack the while!
In bliss he did undo himself;
Where life was full he slew himself—
How could I choose but smile?

Would ye but understand!
Joy is on every hand!
Ye shut your eyes and call it night,
Ye grope and fall in seas of light—
Would ye but understand!

## Heaven

Thou bright mirage, that o'er man's arduous way
    Hast hung in the hot sky, with fountains streaming,
    Cool marble domes, and palm-fronds waving, gleaming,—
Vision of rest and peace to end the day!
Now he is wearied, alone, astray,
    Spent with long labor, led by thy sweet seeming,
    Faint as the breath of Nature's lightest dreaming,
Thou waverest and vanishest away!

Can Nature dream? Is God's great sky deceiving?
　　Where joy like that the clouds above us show
　　Be sure the counterpart must lie below,
Sweeter than hope, more blessed than believing!
　　We lose the fair reflection of our home
　　Because so near its gates our feet have come!


## Ballad of the Summer Sun

It is said that human nature needeth hardship to be strong,
That highest growth has come to man in countries white with snow;
And they tell of truth and wisdom that to northern folk belong,
And claim the brain is feeble where the south winds always blow.
They forget to read the story of the ages long ago:
The lore that built the pyramids where still the simoon[21] veers,
The knowledge framing Tyrian ships,[22] the greater skill that steers,
The learning of the Hindu in his volumes never done,[23]
All the wisdom of Egyptians and the old Chaldean seers,[24]
Came to man in summer lands beneath a summer sun.

It is said that human nature needeth hardship to be strong,
That courage bred of meeting cold makes martial bosoms glow;
And they point to mighty generals the northern folk among,
And call mankind emasculate where southern waters flow.
They forget to look at history and see the nations grow!
The cohorts of Assyrian kings,[25] the Pharaohs' charioteers,[26]
The march of Alexander,[27] the Persians' conquering spears,[28]
The legions of the Romans, from Ethiop to Hun,[29]
The power that mastered all the world and held it years on years,—
Came to man in summer lands beneath a summer sun.

It is said that human nature needeth hardship to be strong,
That only pain and suffering the power to feel bestow;
And they show us noble artists made great by loss and wrong,
And say the soul is lowered that hath pleasure without woe.
They forget the perfect monuments that pleasure's blessings show;
The statue and the temple that no man living nears,
Song and verse and music forever in the ears,
The glory that remaineth while the sands of time shall run,
The beauty of immortal art that never disappears,—
Came to man in summer lands beneath a summer sun.

The faith of Thor and Odin,[30] the creed of force and fears,
Cruel gods that deal in death, the icebound soul reveres,
But the Lord of Peace and Blessing was not one!
Truth and Power and Beauty—Love that endeth tears—
Came to man in summer lands beneath a summer sun.

## Pioneers

Long have we sung our noble pioneers,
    Vanguard of progress, heralds of the time,
    Guardians of industry and art sublime,
Leaders of man down all the brightening years!
To them the danger, to their wives the tears
    While we sit safely in the city's grime,
    In old-world trammels of distress and crime,
Playing with words and thoughts, with doubts and fears.

Children of axe and gun! Ye take to-day
    The baby steps of man's first, feeblest age,
    While we, thought-seekers of the printed page,
We lead the world down its untrodden way!
    Ours the drear wastes and leagues of empty waves,
    The lonely deaths, the undiscovered graves.


## Exiles

Exiled from home. The far sea rolls
Between them and the country of their birth;
The childhood-turning impulse of their souls
    Pulls half across the earth.

Exiled from home. No mother to take care
That they work not too hard, grieve not too sore;
No older brother nor small sister fair;
    No father any more.

Exiled from home; from all familiar things;
The low-browed roof, the grass-surrounded door;
Accustomed labors that gave daylight wings;
    Loved steps on the worn floor.

Exiled from home. Young girls sent forth alone
When most their hearts need close companioning;
No love and hardly friendship may they own,
    No voice of welcoming.

Blinded with homesick tears the exile stands;
To toil for alien household gods she comes;
A servant and a stranger in our lands,
    Homeless within our homes.


## A Nevada Desert[31]

An aching, blinding, barren, endless plain,
    Corpse-colored with white mould of alkali,
Hairy with sage-brush, slimy after rain,

Burnt with the sky's hot scorn, and still again
    Sullenly burning back against the sky.

Dull green, dull brown, dull purple, and dull gray,
    The hard earth white with ages of despair,
Slow-crawling, turbid streams where dead reeds sway,
Low wall of somber mountains fair away,
    And sickly stream of geysers on the air.

## Tree Feelings

I wonder if they like it—being trees?
I suppose they do. . . .
It must feel good to have the ground so flat,
And feel yourself stand right straight up like that—
So stiff in the middle—and then branch at ease,
Big boughs that arch, small ones that bend and blow,
And all those fringy leaves that flutter so.
You'd think they'd break off at the lower end
When the wind fills them, and their great heads bend.
But then you think of all the roots they drop,
As much at bottom as there is on top,—
A double tree, widespread in earth and air
Like a reflection in the water there.

I guess they like to stand still in the sun
And just breathe out and in, and feel the cool sap run;
And like to feel the rain run through their hair
And slide down to the roots and settle there.
But I think they like wind best. From the light touch
That lets the leaves whisper and kiss so much,
To the great swinging, tossing, flying wide,
And all the time so stiff and strong inside!
And the big winds, that pull, and make them feel
How long their roots are, and the earth how leal!

And O the blossoms! And the wild seeds lost!
And jeweled martyrdom of fiery frost!
And fruit trees. I'd forgotten. No cold gem,
But to be apples—and bow down with them!

## Monotony—from California

When ragged lines of passing days go by,
Crowding and hurried, broken-linked and slow,
Some sobbing pitifully as they pass,
Some angry-hot and fierce, some angry cold,
Some raging and some wailing, and again
The fretful days one cannot read aright,—

Then truly, when the fair days smile on us,
We feel that loveliness with sharper touch
And grieve to lose it for the next day's chance.
And so men question—they who never know
If beauty comes or horror, pain or joy—
If we, whose sky is peace, whose hours are glad,
Find not our happiness monotonous!

But when the long procession of the days
Rolls musically down the waiting year,
Close-ranked, rich-robed, flower-garlanded and fair;
Broad brows of peace, deep eyes of soundless truth,
And lips of love—warm, steady, changeless love;
Each one more beautiful, till we forget
Our niggard fear of losing half an hour,
And learn to count on more and ever more,—
In the remembered joy of yesterday,
In the full rapture of to-day's delight,
And knowledge of the happiness to come,
We learn to let life pass without regret,
We learn to hold life softly and in peace,
We learn to meet life gladly, full of faith,
We learn what God is, and to trust in Him!

## The Beds of Fleur-de-Lys

High-lying, sea-blown stretches of green turf,
    Wind-bitten close, salt-colored by the sea,
Low curve on curve spread far to the cool sky,
And, curving over them as long they lie,
        Beds of wild fleur-de-lys.

Wide-flowing, self-sown, stealing near and far,
    Breaking the green like islands in the sea;
Great stretches at your feet, and spots that bend
Dwindling over the horizon's end,—
        Wild beds of fleur-de-lys.

The light keen wind streams on across the lifts,
    Thin winds of western springtime by the sea;
The close turf smiles unmoved, but over her
Is the far-flying rustle and sweet stir
        In beds of fleur-de-lys.

And here and there across the smooth, low grass
    Tall maidens wander, thinking of the sea;
And bend, and bend, with light robes blown aside,
For the blue lily-flowers that bloom so wide,—
        The beds of fleur-de-lys.

## It is Good to be Alive

It is good to be alive when the trees shine green,
And the steep red hills stand up against the sky;
Big sky, blue sky, with flying clouds between—
It is good to be alive and see the clouds drive by!

It is good to be alive when the strong winds blow,
The strong, sweet winds blowing straightly off the sea;
Great sea, green sea, with swinging ebb and flow—
It is good to be alive and see the waves roll free!

## The Changeless Year—Southern California

Doth Autumn remind thee of sadness?
And Winter of wasting and pain?
Midsummer, of joy that was madness?
    Spring, of hope that was vain?

Do the Seasons fly fast at thy laughter?
Do the Seasons lag slow if thou weep,
Till thou long'st for the land lying after
    The River of Sleep?[32]

Come here, where the West lieth golden
In the light of an infinite sun,
Where Summer doth Winter embolden
    Till they reign here as one!

Here the Seasons tread soft and steal slowly;
A moment of question and doubt—
Is it Winter? Come faster!—come wholly!—
    And Spring rusheth out!

We forget there are tempests and changes;
We forget there are days that are drear;
In a dream of delight, the soul ranges
    Through the measureless year.

Still the land is with blosoms enfolden,
Still the sky burnest blue in its deeps;
Time noddeth, 'mid poppies all golden,
    And memory sleeps.

## Where Memory Sleeps—Rondeau

Where memory sleeps the soul doth rise,
Free of that past where sorrow lies,
    And storeth against future ills
    The courage of the constant hills,
The comfort of the quiet skies.

Fair is this land to tired eyes,
Where summer sunlight never dies,
    And summer's peace the spirit fills,
      Where memory sleeps.

Safe from the season's changing cries
And chill of yearly sacrifice,
    Great roses crowd the window-sills,—
    Calm roses that no winter kills.
The peaceful heart all pain denies,
      Where memory sleeps.

## California Car Windows

Lark songs ringing to heaven,
    Earth light clear as the sky,
Air like the breath of a greenhouse
    With the greenhouse roof on high.

Flowers to see till you are weary,
    To travel in hours and hours;
Ranches of gold and purple,
    Counties covered with flowers.

A rainbow, a running rainbow
    That flies at our side for hours;
A ribbon, a broidered ribbon,
    A rainbow ribbon of flowers!

## Limits

On sand—loose sand and shifting—
On sand—dry sand and drifting—
    The city grows to the west;
Not till its border reaches
The ocean-beaten beaches
    Will it rest.

On hills—steep hills and lonely,
That stop at cloudland only—
    The city climbs to the sky;
Not till the souls who make it
Touch the clear light and take it,
    Will it die.

## Powell Street[33]

You start
From the town's hot heart

To ride up Powell Street.
Hotel and theatre and crowding shops,[34]
And market's cabled stream that never stops,
And the mixed hurrying beat
Of countless feet—
Take a front seat.
Before you rise
Six terraced hills, up to the low-hung skies;
Low where across the hill they seem to lie,
And then—how high!
Up you go slowly. To the right
A wide square, green and bright.[35]
Above that green a broad façade,
Strongly and beautifully made,
In warm clear color standeth fair and true
Against the blue.
Only, above, two purple domes rise bold,[36]
Twin-budded spires, bright-tipped with balls of gold.
Past that, and up you glide,
Up, up, till, either side,
Wide earth and water stretch around—away—
The straits, the hills, and the low-lying, wide-spread, dusky bay.
Great houses here,
Dull, opulent, severe.[37]
Dives' gold birds on guarding lamps a-wing[38]—
Dead gold, that may not sing!
Fair on the other side
Smooth, steep-laid sweeps of turf and green boughs waving wide.
This is the hilltop's crown.[39]
Below you, down
In blurred, dim streets, the market quarter lies,[40]
Foul, narrow, torn with cries
Of tortured things in cages, and the smell
Of daily bloodshed rising; that is hell.

But up here on the crown of Powell Street
The air is sweet;
And the green swaying mass of eucalyptus bends
Like hands of friends,
To gladden you despite the mansions' frown.
Then you go down.

Down, down, and round the turns to lower grades;
Lower in all ways; darkening with the shades
Of poverty, old youth, and unearned age,
And that quick squalor which so blots the page
Of San Francisco's beauty,—swift decay
Chasing the shallow grandeur of a day.

Here, like a noble lady of lost state,
Still calmly smiling at encroaching fate,
Amidst the squalor, rises Russian Hill,[41]
Proud, isolated, lonely, lovely still.

So on you glide.
Till the blue straits lie wide
Before you; purple mountains loom across,[42]
And islands green as moss;[43]
With soft white fog-wreaths drifting, drifting through
To comfort you;
And light, low-singing waves that tell you reach
The end—North Beach.[44]

## From Russian Hill

A strange day—bright and still;
Strange for the stillness here,
For the strong trade-winds blow
With such a steady sweep it seems like rest,
Forever steadily across the crest
    Of Russian Hill.

Still now and clear,—
So clear you count the houses spreading wide
In the fair cities on the farther side
Of our broad bay;[45]
And brown Goat Island lieth large between,[46]
Its brownness brightening into sudden green
    From rains of yesterday.

Blue? Blue above of California sky,
Which has no peer on earth of its pure flame;
Bright blue of bay and strait spread wide below,
And, past the low, dull hills that hem it so,—
Blue as the sky, blue as the placid bay,—
    Blue mountains far away.

Thanks this year for the early rains that came
To bless us, meaning Summer by and by.
This is our Spring-in-Autumn, making one
The Indian Summer tenderness of sun—
Its hazy stillness, and soft far-heard sound—
And the sweet riot of abundant spring,
The greenness flaming out from everything,
    The sense of coming gladness in the ground.

From this high peace and purity look down;
Between you and the blueness lies the town.
Under those huddled roofs the heart of man

Beats warmer than this brooding day,
Spreads wider than the hill-rimmed bay,
And throbs to tenderer life, were it but seen,
    Than all this new-born, all-enfolding green!

Within that heart lives still
All that one guesses, dreams, and sees—
Sitting in sunlight, warm, at ease—
From this high island,—Russian Hill.

### "An Unusual Rain"

Again!
Another day of rain!
It has rained for years.
It never clears.
The clouds come down so low
They drag and drip
Across each hill-top's tip.
In progress slow
They blow in from the sea
Eternally;
Hang heavily and black,
And then roll back;
And rain and rain and rain,
Both drifting in and drifting out again.

They come down to the ground,
These clouds, where the ground is high;
And, lest the weather fiend forget
And leave one hidden spot unwet,
The fog comes up to the sky!
And all our pavement of planks and logs
Reeks with the rain and steeps in the fogs
Till the water rises and sinks and presses
Into your bonnets and shoes and dresses;
And every outdoor-going dunce
Is wet in forty ways at once

Wet?
It's wetter than being drowned.
Dark?
Such darkness never was found
Since first the light was made. And cold?
O come to the land of grapes and gold,
Of fruit and flowers and sunshine gay,
When the rainy season's under way!

And they tell you calmly, evermore,
They never had such rain before!

What's that you say? Come out?
Why, see that sky!
Oh, what a world! so clear! so high!
So clean and lovely all about;
The sunlight burning through and through,
And everything just blazing blue.
And look! the whole world blossoms again
The minute the sunshine follows the rain.
Warm sky—earth basking under—
Did it ever rain, I wonder?

## The Hills

The flowing waves of our warm sea
    Roll to the beach and die,
But the soul of the waves forever fills
The curving crests of our restless hills
    That climb so wantonly.

Up and up till you look to see
    Along the cloud-kissed top
The great hill-breakers curve and comb
In crumbling lines of falling foam
    Before they settle and drop.

Down and down, with the shuddering sweep
    Of the sea-wave's glassy wall,
You sink with a plunge that takes your breath,
A shrill the stirreth and quickeneth,
    Like the great line steamer's fall.

We have laid our streets by the square and line,
    We have built by the line and square;
But the strong hill-rises arch below
And force the houses to curve and flow
    In lines of beauty there.

And off to the north and east and south,
    With wildering mists between,
They ring us round with wavering hold,
With fold on fold of rose and gold,
    Violet, azure, and green.

## City's Beauty

Fair, oh, fair are the hills uncrowned,
    Only wreathed and garlanded
    With the soft clouds overhead,
With the waving streams of rain;

Fair in golden sunlight drowned,
  Bathed and buried in the bright
  Warm luxuriance of light,—
Fair the hills without a stain.

Fairer far the hills should stand
  Crownèd with a city's halls,
  With the glimmer of white walls,
With the climbing grace of towers;
Fair with great fronts tall and grand,
  Stately streets that meet the sky,
  Lovely roof-lines, low and high,—
Fairer for the days and hours.

Woman's beauty fades and flies,
  In the passing of the years,
  With the falling of the tears,
With the lines of toil and stress;
City's beauty never dies,—
  Never while her people know
  How to love and honor so
Her immortal loveliness.


## Two Skies—from England

They have a sky in Albion,⁴⁷
  At least they tell me so;
But she will wear a veil so thick,
And she does have the sulks so quick,
  And weeps so long and slow,
  That one can hardly know.

Yes, there's a sky in Albion.
  She's shown herself of late.
And where it was not white or gray,
It was quite bluish—in a way;
  But near and full of weight,
  Like an overhanging plate!

Our sky in California!
  Such light the angels knew,
When the strong, tender smile of God
Kindled the spaces where they trod,
  And made all life come true!
  Deep, soundless, burning blue!


## Winds and Leaves—from England

Wet winds that flap the sodden leaves!
Wet leaves that drop and fall!

Unhappy, leafless trees the wind bereaves!
     Poor trees and small!

All of a color, solemn in your green;
All of a color, somber in your brown;
All of a color, dripping gray between
     When leaves are down!

O for the bronze-green eucalyptus spires
Far-flashing up against the endless blue!
Shifting and glancing in the steady fires
     Of sun and moonlight too.

Dark orange groves! Pomegranate hedges bright,
And varnished fringes of the pepper trees!
And O that wind of sunshine! Wind of light!
     Wind of Pacific seas!

## On the Pawtuxet[48]

Broad and blue is the river, all bright in the sun;
The little waves sparkle, the little waves run;
The birds carol high, and the winds whisper low;
The boats beckon temptingly, row upon row;
Her hand is in mine as I help her step in.
Please Heaven, this day I shall lose or shall win—
     Broad and blue is the river.

Cool and gray is the river, the sun sinks apace,
And the rose-colored twilight glows soft in her face.
In the midst of the rose-color Venus doth shine,[49]
And the blossoming wild grapes are sweeter than wine;
Tall trees rise above us, four bridges are past,
And my stroke's running slow as the current runs fast—
     Cool and gray is the river.

Smooth and black is the river, no sound as we float
Save the soft-lapping water in under the boat.
The whites mists are rising, the moon's rising too,
And Venus, triumphant, rides high in the blue.
I hold the shawl round her, her hand is in mine,
And we drift under grape-blossoms sweeter than wine—
     Smooth and black is the river.

## A Moonrise

The heavy mountains, lying huge and dim,
With uncouth outline breaking heaven's brim;
And while I watched and waited, o'er them soon,
Cloudy, enormous, spectral, rose the moon.

# Their Grass!—A Protest from California

They say we have no grass!
To hear them talk
You'd think that grass could walk
And was their bosom friend,—no day to pass
Between them and their grass.

"No grass!" they say who live
Where hot bricks give
The hot stones all their heat and back again,—
A baking hell for men.
"O, but," they haste to say, "we have our parks,
Where fat policemen check the children's larks;
And sign to sign repeats as in a glass,
'Keep off the grass!'
We have our cities' parks and grass, you see!"
Well—so have we!

But 'tis the country that they sing of most. "Alas,"
They sing, "for our wide acres of soft grass!—
To please us living and to hide us dead—"
You'd think Walt Whitman's first was all they read![50]
You'd think they all went out upon the quiet
Nebuchadnezzar to outdo in diet![51]
You'd think they found no other green thing fair,
Even its seed an honor in their hair!
You'd think they had this bliss the whole year round,—
Evergreen grass!—and we, ploughed ground!

But come now, how does earth's pet plumage grow
Under your snow?
Is your beloved grass as softly nice
When packed in ice?
For six long months you live beneath a blight,—
No grass in sight.
You bear up bravely. And not only that,
But leave your grass and travel; and thereat
We marvel deeply, with slow western mind,
Wondering within us what these people find
Among our common oranges and palms
To tear them from the well-remembered charms
Of their dear vegetable. But still they come,
Frost-bitten invalids! to our bright home,
And chide our grasslessness! Until we say,
"But if you hate it so, why come? Why stay?
Just go away!
Go to—your grass!"

## The Prophets

Time was we stoned the Prophets. Age on age,
When men were strong to save, the world hath slain them.
People are wiser now; they waste no rage—
    The Prophets entertain them!

## Similar Cases

There was once a little animal,
No bigger than a fox,
And on five toes he scampered
Over Tertiary rocks.
They called him Eohippus,[52]
And they called him very small,
And they thought him of no value—
When they thought of him at all;
For the lumpish old Dinoceras[53]
And Coryphodon[54] so slow
Were the heavy aristocracy
In days of long ago.

Said the little Eohippus,
"I am going to be a horse!
And on my middle finger-nails
To run my earthly course!
I'm going to have a flowing tail!
I'm going to have a mane!
I'm going to stand fourteen hands high
On the psychozoic[55] plain!"

The Coryphodon was horrified,
The Dinoceras was shocked;
And they chased young Eohippus,
But he skipped away and mocked.
And they laughed enormous laughter,
And they groaned enormous groans,
And they bade young Eohippus
Go view his father's bones.
Said they, "You always were as small
And mean as now we see,
And that's conclusive evidence
That you're always going to be.
What! Be a great, tall, handsome beast,
With hoofs to gallop on?
Why! You'd have to change your nature!"
Said the Loxolophodon.[56]

They considered him disposed of,
And retired with gait serene;
That was the way they argued
In "the early Eocene."[57]

There was once an Anthropoidal Ape,
Far smarter than the rest,
And everything that they could do
He always did the best;
So they naturally disliked him,
And they gave him shoulders cool,
And when they had to mention him
They said he was a fool.

Cried this pretentious Ape one day,
"I'm going to be a Man!
And stand upright, and hunt, and fight,
And conquer all I can!
I'm going to cut down forest trees,
To make my houses higher!
I'm going to kill the Mastodon![58]
I'm going to make a fire!"

Loud screamed the Anthropoidal Apes
With laughter wild and gay;
They tried to catch that boastful one,
But he always got away.
So they yelled at him in chorus,
Which he minded not a whit;
And they pelted him with cocoanuts,
Which didn't seem to hit.
And then they gave him reasons
Which they thought of much avail,
To prove how his preposterous
Attempt was sure to fail.
Said the sages, "In the first place,
The thing cannot be done!
And, second, if it could be,
It would not be any fun!
And, third, and most conclusive,
And admitting no reply,
You would have to change your nature!
We should like to see you try!"
They chuckled then triumphantly,
These lean and hairy shapes,
For these things passed as arguments
With the Anthropoidal Apes.

There was once a Neolithic Man,[59]
An enterprising wight,
Who made his chopping implements
Unusually bright.
Unusually clever he,
Unusually brave,
And he drew delightful Mammoths
On the borders of his cave.[60]
To his Neolithic neighbors,
Who were startled and surprised,
Said he, "My friends, in course of time,
We shall be civilized!
We are going to live in cities!
We are going to fight in wars!
We are going to eat three times a day
Without the natural cause!
We are going to turn life upside down
About a thing called gold!
We are going to want the earth, and take
As much as we can hold!
We are going to wear great piles of stuff
Outside our proper skins!
We are going to have diseases!
And Accomplishments!! And Sins!!!"

Then they all rose up in fury
Against their boastful friend,
For prehistoric patience
Cometh quickly to an end.
Said one, "This is chimerical!
Utopian! Absurd!"
Said another, "What a stupid life!
Too dull, upon my word!"
Cried all, "Before such things can come,
You idiotic child,
You must alter Human Nature!"
And they all sat back and smiled.
Thought they, "An answer to that last
It will be hard to find!"
It was a clinching argument
To the Neolithic Mind!


### A Conservative[61]

The garden beds I wandered by
One bright and cheerful morn,
When I found a new-fledged butterfly

A-sitting on a thorn,
A black and crimson butterfly,
All doleful and forlorn.

I thought that life could have no sting
To infant butterflies,
So I gazed on this unhappy thing
With wonder and surprise,
While sadly with his waving wing
He wiped his weeping eyes.

Said I, "What can the matter be?
Why weepest thou so sore?
With garden fair and sunlight free
And flowers in goodly store—"
But he only turned away from me
And burst into a roar.

Cried he, "My legs are thin and few
Where once I had a swarm!
Soft fuzzy fur—a joy to view—
Once kept my body warm,
Before these flapping wing-things grew,
To hamper and deform!"

At that outrageous bug I shot
The fury of mine eye;
Said I, in scorn all burning hot,
In rage and anger high,
"You ignominious idiot!
Those wings are made to fly!"

"I do not want to fly," said he,
"I only want to squirm!"
And he drooped his wings dejectedly,
But still his voice was firm:
"I do not want to be a fly!
I want to be a worm!"

O yesterday of unknown lack!
To-day of unknown bliss!
I left my fool in red and black,
The last I saw was this,—
The creature madly climbing back
Into his chrysalis.

## An Obstacle

I was climbing up a mountain-path
    With many things to do,

Important business of my own,
　　And other people's too,
When I ran against a Prejudice
　　That quite cut off the view.

My work was such as could not wait,
　　My path quite clearly showed,
My strength and time were limited,
　　I carried quite a load;
And there that hulking Prejudice
　　Sat all across the road.

So I spoke to him politely,
　　For he was huge and high,
And begged that he would move a bit
　　And let me travel by.
He smiled, but as for moving!—
　　He didn't even try.

And then I reasoned quietly
　　With that colossal mule:
My time was short—no other path—
　　The mountain winds were cool.
I argued like a Solomon;[62]
　　He sat there like a fool.

Then I flew into a passion,
　　I danced and howled and swore.
I pelted and belabored him
　　Till I was stiff and sore;
He got as mad as I did—
　　But he sat there as before.

And then I begged him on my knees;
　　I might be kneeling still
If so I hoped to move that mass
　　Of obdurate ill-will—
As well invite the monument
　　To vacate Bunker Hill![63]

So I sat before him helpless,
　　In an ecstasy of woe—
The mountain mists were rising fast,
　　The sun was sinking slow—
When a sudden inspiration came,
　　As sudden winds do blow.

I took my hat, I took my stick,
　　My load I settled fair,

I approached that awful incubus
    With an absent-minded air—
And I walked directly through him,
    As if he wasn't there!

## The Fox who had Lost his Tail[64]

The fox who had lost his tail found out
    That now he could faster go;
He had less to cover when hid for prey,
He had less to carry on hunting day,
He had less to guard when he stood at bay;
    He was really better so!

Now he was a fine altruistical fox
    With the good of his race at heart,
So he ran to his people with tailless speed,
To tell of the change they all must need,
And recommend as a righteous deed
    That they and their tails should part!

Plain was the gain as plain could be,
    But his words did not avail;
For they all replied, "We perceive your case;
You do not speak for the good of the race,
But only to cover your own disgrace,
    Because you have lost your tail!"

Then another fox, of a liberal mind,
    With a tail of splendid size,
Became convinced that the tailless state
Was better for all of them, soon or late.
Said he, "I will let my own tail wait,
    And so I can open their eyes."

Plain was the gain as plain could be,
    But his words did not avail,
For they all made answer, "My plausible friend,
You talk wisely and well, but you talk to no end.
We know you're dishonest and only pretend,
    For you have not lost your tail!"

## The Sweet Uses of Adversity

In Norway fiords, in summer-time,
    The Norway birch is fair:
The white trunks shine, the green leaves twine,
The whole tree growth tall and fine;

For all it wants is there,—
Water and warmth and air,—
Full fed in all its nature needs, and showing
That nature is perfection by its growing.

But follow the persistent tree
To the limit of endless snow
There you may see what a birch can be!
The product showeth plain and free
How nobly plants can grow
With nine months' winter slow.
'Tis fitted to survive in that position,
Developed by the force of bad condition.

See now what life the tree doth keep,—
Branchless, three-leaved, and tough;
In June the leaf-buds peep, flowers in July dare creep
To bloom, the fruit in August, and then sleep.
Strong is the tree and rough,
It lives, and that's enough.
"Dog's ear" the name the peasants call it by—
A Norway birch—and less than one inch high!
. . . . . . . .

That silver monarch of the summer wood,
Tall, straight, and lovely, rich in all things good,
Knew not in his perversity
The sweet uses of adversity.


## Connoisseurs

"No," said the Cultured Critic, gazing haughtily
Whereon some untrained brush had wandered naughtily,
From canons free;
"Work such as this lacks value and perspective,
Has no real feeling,—inner or reflective,—
Does not appeal to me."

Then quoth the vulgar, knowing art but meagerly,
Their unbesought opinions airing eagerly,
"What, ain't that flat?"
Voicing their ignorance all unconcernedly,
Saying of what the Critic scorned so learnedly,
"I don't like that!"

The Critic now vouchsafed approval sparingly
Of what some genius had attempted daringly,
"This fellow tries;
He handles his conception frankly, feelingly.
Such work as this, done strongly and appealingly,
I recognize."

The vulgar, gazing widely and unknowingly,
Still volunteered their cheap impressions flowingly,
    "Oh, come and see!"
But all that they could say of art's reality
Was this poor voice of poorer personality,
    "Now, that suits me!"


## Technique

Cometh to-day the very skilful man;
    Profoundly skilful in his chosen art;
All things that other men can do he can,
    And so them better. He is very smart.

Sayeth, "My work is here before you all;
    Come now with duly cultured mind to view it.
Here is great work, no part of it is small;
    Perceive how well I do it!

"I do it to perfection. Studious years
    Were spent to reach the pinnacle I've won;
Labor and thought are in my work, and tears.
    Behold how well 'tis done!

"See with what power this great effect is shown;
    See with what ease you get the main idea;
A master in my art, I stand alone;
    Now you may praise,—I hear."

And I, O master, I perceive your sway,
    I note the years of study, toil, and strain
That brought the easy power you wield to-day,
    The height you now attain.

"Freely your well-trained power I see you spend,
    Such skill in all my life I never saw;
You have done nobly; but, my able friend,
    What have you done it for?

"You have no doubt achieved your dearest end:
    Your work is faultless to the cultured view.
You do it well, but, O my able friend,
    What is it that you do?"


## The Pastellette[65]

"The pastille is too strong," said he
    "Lo! I will make it fainter yet!"
And he wrought with tepid ecstasy
    A pastellette.

A touch—a word—a tone half caught—
    He softly felt and handled them;
Flavor of feeling—scent of thought—
    Shimmer of gem—

That we may read, and feel as he
    What vague, pale pleasure we can get
From this mild, witless mystery,—
    The pastellette.


## The Pig and the Pearl

Said the Pig to the Pearl, "Oh, fie!
Tasteless, and hard, and dry—
    Get out of my sty!

Glittering, smooth, and clean,
You only seek to be seen!
I am dirty and big!
A virtuous, valuable pig.
For me all things are sweet
That I can possibly eat;
But you—how can you be good
Without being fit for food?
Not even food for me,
Who can eat all this you see,
No matter how foul and sour;
I revel from hour to hour
In refuse of great and small;
But you are no good at all,
And if I should gulp you, quick,
It would probably make me sick!"
Said the Pig to the Pearl, "Oh, fie!"
And she rooted her out of the sty.

A Philosopher chancing to pass
Saw the Pearl in the grass,
And laid hand on the same in a trice,
For the Pearl was a Pearl of Great Price.[66]
Said he, "Madame Pig, if you knew
What a fool thing you do,
It would grieve even you!
Grant that pearls are not just to your taste,
Must you let them run waste?
You care only for hogwash, I know,
For your litter and you. Even you,
This tasteless hard thing which you scorn
Would buy acres of corn;

And apples, and pumpkins, and pease,
By the ton, if you please!
By the wealth which this pearl represents,
You could grow so immense—
You, and every last one of your young—
That your fame would be sung
As the takes of every first prize,
For your flavor and size!
From even a Pig's point of view
The Pearl was worth millions to you.
Be a Pig—and a fool—(you must be them)
But try to know Pearls when you see them!"

## Poor Human Nature

    I saw a meager, melancholy cow,
Bless with a starveling calf that sucked in vain;
    Eftsoon he died. I asked the mother how—?
Quoth she, "Of every four there dieth twain!"
        Poor bovine nature!

I saw a sickly horse of shambling gait,
    Ugly and wicked, weak in leg and back,
Useless in all ways, in a wretched state.
    "We're all poor creatures!" said the sorry hack.
        Poor equine nature!

I saw a slow cat crawling on the ground,
    Weak, clumsy, inefficient, full of fears,
The mice escaping from her aimless bound.
    Moaned she, "This truly is a vale of tears!"
        Poor feline nature!

Then did I glory in my noble race,
    Healthful and beautiful, alert and strong,
Rejoicing that we held a higher place
    And need not add to their our mournful song,—
        Poor human nature!

## Our San Francisco Climate

Said I to my friend from the East,—
    A tenderfoot he,—
And I showed him the greatest and least
    Of our hills by the sea,
"How do you like our climate?"
    And I smiled in my glee.

I showed him the blue of the hills,
       And the blue of the sky,
And the blue of the beautiful bay
       Where the ferry-boats ply;
And "How do you like our climate?"
       Securely asked I.

Then the wind blew over the sand,
       And the fog came down,
And the papers and dust were on hand
       All over the town.
"How do you like our climate?"
       I cried with a frown.

On the corner we stood as we met
       Awaiting a car;
Beneath us a vent-hole was set,
       As our street corners are—
And street corners in our San Francisco
       Are perceptible far.

He meant to have answered, of course,
       I could see that he tried;
But he had not the strength of a horse,
       And before he replied
The climate rose up from that corner in force,
       And he died!


## Criticism

The Critic eyed the sunset as the umber turned to gray,
       Slow fading in the somewhat foggy west;
To the color-cultured Critic 'twas a very dull display,
"'Tisn't half so good a sunset as was offered yesterday!
I wonder why," he murmured, as he sadly turned away
       "The sunsets can't be always at their best!"


## Another Creed

Another creed! We're all so pleased!
A gentle, tentative new creed. We're eased
Of all those things we could not quite believe,
But would not give the lie to. Now perceive
How charmingly this suits us! Science even
Has naught against our modern views of Heaven;
And yet the most emotional of women
May find this creed a warm, deep sea to swim in.

Here's something now so loose and large of fit
That all the churches may come under it,

And we may see upon the earth once more
A church united,—as we had before!
Before so much of precious blood was poured
That each in his own way might serve the Lord!
All wide divergence in sweet union sunk,
Like branches growing up into a trunk!

And in our intellectual delight
In this sweet formula that sets us right;
And controversial exercises gay
With those who still prefer a differing way;
And our glad effort to make known this wonder
And get all others to unite there under,—
We, joying in this newest, best of creeds,
Continue still to do our usual deeds!

## The Little Lion

It was a little lion lay—
In wait he lay—he lay in wait.
Came those who said, "Pray come my way;
We joy to see a lion play,
        And laud his gait!"

The little lion mildly came—
In wait for prey—for prey in wait.
The people all adored his name,
And those who led him saw the same
        With hearts elate.

The little lion grew that day,—
In glee he went—he went in glee,
Said he, "I love to seek my prey,
But also love to see the way
        My prey seek me!"

## A Misfit

O Lord, take me out of this!
        I do not fit!
My body does not suit my mind,
My brain is weak in the knees and blind,
My clothes are not what I want to find—
        Not one bit!

My house is not the house I like—
        Not one bit!
My church is built so loose and thin
That ten fall out where one falls in;

My creed is buttoned with a pin—
    It does not fit!

The school I went to wasn't right—
    Not one bit!
The education given me
Was meant for the community,
And my poor head works differently—
    It does not fit!

I try to move and find I can't—
    Not one bit!
Things that were given me to stay
Are mostly lost and blown away,
And what I have to use to-day—
    It does not fit!

What I was taught I cannot do—
    Not one bit!
And what I do I was not taught
And what I find I have not sought;
I never say the thing I ought—
    It does not fit!

I have not meant to be like this—
    Not one bit!
But in the puzzle and the strife
I fail my friend and pain my wife;
Oh, how it hurts to have a life
    That does not fit!

## On New Year's Day

On New Year's Day he plans a cruise
To Heaven straight—no time to lose!
    Vowing to live so virtuously
    That each besetting sin shall flee—
Good resolutions wide he strews
    On New Year's Day.

A while he minds his p's and q's,
And all temptations doth refuse,
    Recalling his resolves so free
    On New Year's Day.

But in the long year that ensures,
They fade away by threes and twos—
    The place we do not wish to see
    Is paved with all he meant to be,
When he next year his life reviews—
    On New Year's Day.

## Our East

Our East, long looking backward over sea,
In loving study of what used to be,
Has grown to treat our West with the same scorn
England has had for us since we were born.

You'd think to hear this Eastern judgment hard
The West was just New England's back yard!
That all the West was made for, last and least,
Was to raise pork and wheat to feed the East!

A place to travel in, for rest and health,
A place to struggle in and get the wealth,
The only normal end of which, of course,
Is to return to its historic source!

Our Western acres, curving to the sun,
The Western strength whereby our work is done,
All Western progress, they attribute fair
To Eastern Capital invested there!

New England never liked old England's scorn
Do they think theirs more easy to be borne?
Or that the East, Britain's rebellious child,
Will find the grandson, West, more meek and mild?

In union still our sovereignty has stood,
A union formed with prayer and sealed with blood.
We stand together. Patience, mighty West!
Don't mind this scolding from your last year's nest!


## Unmentionable[67]

There is a thing of which I fain would speak,
    Yet shun the deed;
Lest hot disgust flush the averted cheek
    Of those who read.

And yet it is as common in our sight
    As dust or grass;
Loathed by the lifted skirt, the tiptoe light,
    Of those who pass.

We say no word, but the big placard rests
    Frequent in view,
To sicken those who do not with requests
    Of those who do.

"Gentleman will not," the mild placards say.
    They read with scorn.

"Gentlemen must not"—they defile the way
    Of those who warn.

On boat and car the careful lady lifts
    Her dress aside;
If careless—think, fair traveller of the gifts
    Of those who ride!

On every hall and sidewalk, floor and stair,
    Where man's at home,
This loathsomeness is added to the care
    Of those who come.

As some foul slug his trail of slime displays
    On leaf and stalk,
These street-beasts make a horror in the ways
    Of those who walk.

We cannot ask reform of those who do—
    They can't or won't.
We can express the scorn, intense and true,
    Of those who don't.


## An Invitation from California

Aren't you tired of protection from the weather?
    Of defences, guards, and shields?
Aren't you tired of the worry as to whether
    This year the farm land yields?

Aren't you tired of the wetness and the dryness,
    The dampness, and the hotness, and the cold?
Of waiting on the weather man with shyness
    To see if the last plans hold?

Aren't you tired of the doctoring and nursing,
    Of the "sickly winters" and the pocket pills,—
Tired of sorrowing, and burying, and cursing
    At Providence and undertakers' bills?

Aren't you tired of all the threatening and doubting,
    The "weather-breeder"[68] with its lovely lie;
The dubiety of any sort of outing;
    The chip upon the shoulder of the sky?

Like a beaten horse who dodges your caresses,
    Like a child abused who ducks before your frown,
Is the northerner in our warm air that blesses—
    O come and live and take your elbow down!

Don't be afraid; you do not need defences;
    This heavenly day breeds not a stormy end;

Lay down your arms! cut off your war expenses!
    This weather is your friend!

A friendliness from earth, a joy from heaven,
    A peace that wins your frightened soul at length;
A place where rest as well as work is given,—
    Rest is the food of strength.


## Resolve

To keep my health!
To do my work!
To live!
To see to it I grow and gain and give!
Never to look behind me for an hour!
To wait in weakness, and to walk in power;
But always fronting onward to the light,
Always and always facing toward the right.
Robbed, starved, defeated, fallen, wide astray—
On, with what strength I have!
Back to the way!

&#10019; **WOMAN** &#10019;

## She Walketh Veiled and Sleeping

She walketh veiled and sleeping,
For she knoweth not her power;
She obeyeth but the pleading
Of her heart, and the high leading
Of her soul, unto this hour.
Slow advancing, halting, creeping,
Comes the Woman to the hour!—
She walketh veiled and sleeping,
For she knoweth not her power.

## To Man

In dark and early ages, through the primal forests faring,
Ere the soul came shining into prehistoric night,
Two-fold man[1] was equal; they were comrades dear and daring,
Living wide and free together in unreasoning delight.

Ere the soul was born and consciousness came slowly,
Ere the soul was born, to man and woman too,
Ere he found the Tree of Knowledge,[2] that awful tree and holy,
Ere he knew he felt, and knew he knew.

Then he said to Pain, "I am wise now, and I know you!
No more will I suffer while power and wisdom last!"
Then said he to Pleasure, "I am strong, and I will show you
That the will of man can seize you; aye, and hold you fast!"

Food he ate for pleasure, and wine he drank for gladness,
And woman? Ah, the woman! the crown of all delight!—
His now—he knew it! He was strong to madness
In that early dawning after prehistoric night.

His—his forever! That glory sweet and tender!
Ah, but he would love her! And she should love but him!
He would work and struggle for her, he would shelter and defend her;
She should never leave him, never, till their eyes in death were dim.

Close, close he bound her, that she should leave him never;
Weak still he kept her, lest she be strong to flee;
And the fainting flame of passion he kept alive forever
With all the arts and forces of earth and sky and sea.

And, ah, the long journey! The slow and awful ages
They have labored up together, blind and crippled, all astray!
Through what a mighty volume, with a million shameful pages,
From the freedom of the forest to the prisons of to-day!

Food he ate for pleasure, and it slew him with diseases!
Wine he drank for gladness, and it led the way to crime!

And woman? He will hold her—he will have her when he pleases—
And he never once hath seen her since the prehistoric time!

Gone the friend and comrade of the day when life was younger,
She who rests and comforts, she who helps and saves;
Still he seeks her vainly, with a never-dying hunger;
Alone beneath his tyrants, alone above his slaves!

Toiler, bent and weary with the load of thine own making!
Thou who art sad and lonely, though lonely all in vain!
Who hast sought to conquer Pleasure and have her for the taking,
And found that Pleasure only was another name for Pain,—

Nature hath reclaimed thee, forgiving dispossession!
God hath not forgotten, though man doth still forget!
The woman-soul is rising, in despite of thy transgression;
Loose her now—and trust her! She will love thee yet!

Love thee? She will love thee as only freedom knoweth;
Love thee? She will love thee while Love itself doth live!
Fear not the heart of woman! No bitterness it showeth!
The ages of her sorrow have but taught her to forgive!

## Women of To-day

You women of today who fear so much
The women of the future, showing how
The dangers of her course are such and such—
    What are you now?

Mothers and Wives and Housekeepers, forsooth!
Great names! you cry, full scope to rule and please!
Room for wise age and energetic youth!—
    But are you these?

Housekeepers? Do you then, like those of yore,
Keep house with power and pride, with grace and ease?
No, you keep servants only! What is more,
    You don't keep these!

Wives, say you? Wives! Blessed indeed are they
Who hold of love the everlasting keys,
Keeping your husbands' hearts! Alas the day!
    You don't keep these!

And mothers? Pitying Heaven! Mark the cry
From cradle death-beds! Mothers on their knees!
Why, half the children born—as children, die!
    You don't keep these!

And still the wailing babies come and go,
And homes are waste, and husband's hearts fly far;

There is no hope until you dare to know
    The thing you are!

## To the Young Wife

Are you content, you pretty three-years' wife?
    Are you content and satisfied to live
On what your loving husband loves to give,
        And give to him your life?

Are you content with work,—to toil alone,
    To clean things dirty and to soil things clean;
    To be a kitchen-maid, be called a queen,—
        Queen of a cook-stove throne?

Are you content to reign in that small space—
    A wooden palace and a yard-fenced land—
    With other queens abundant on each hand,
        Each fastened in her place?

Are you content to rear your children so?
    Untaught yourself, untrained, perplexed, distressed,
    Are you so sure your way is always best?
        That you can always know?

Have you forgotten how you used to long
    In days of ardent girlhood, to be great,
    To help the groaning world, to serve the state,
        To be so wise—so strong?

And are you quite convinced this is the way,
    The only way a woman's duty lies—
    Knowing all women so have shut their eyes?
        Seeing the world to-day?

Have you no dream of life in fuller store?
    Of growing to be more than that you are?
    Doing the things you now do better far,
        Yet doing others—more?

Losing no love, but finding as you grew
    That as you entered upon nobler life
    You so became a richer, sweeter wife,
        A wiser mother too?

What holds you? Ah, my dear, it is your throne,
    Your paltry queenship in that narrow place,
    Your antique labors, your restricted space,
        Your working all alone!

Be not deceived! 'Tis not your wifely bond
    That holds you, nor the mother's royal power,

But selfish, slavish service hour by hour—
    A life with no beyond!

## False Play

"Do you love me?" asked the mother of her child,
    And the baby answered, "No!"
Great Love listened and sadly smiled;
He knew the love in the heart of the child—
    That you could not wake it so.

"Do not love me?" the foolish mother cried,
    And the baby answered, "No!"
He knew the worth of the trick she tried—
Great Love listened, and grieving, sighed
    That the mother scorned him so.

"Oh, poor mama!" and she played her part
    Till the baby's strength gave way:
He knew it was false in his inmost heart,
But he could not bear that her tears should start,
    So he joined in the lying play.

"Then love mama!" and the soft lips crept
    To the kiss that his love should show,—
The mouth to speak while the spirit slept!
Great Love listened, and blushed, and wept
    That they blasphemed him so.

## Motherhood

Motherhood: First mere laying of an egg,
With blind foreseeing of the wisest place,
And blind provision of the proper food
For unseen larva to grow fat upon
After the instinct-guided mother died,—
Posthumous motherhood, no love, no joy.

Motherhood: Brooding patient o'er the nest,
With gentle stirring of an unknown love;
Defending eggs unhatched, feeding the young
For days of callow feebleness, and then
Driving the fledglings from the nest to fly.

Motherhood: When the kitten and the cub
Cried out alive, the first the mother knew
The fumbling of furry little paws,
The pressure of the hungry little mouths
Against the more than ready mother-breast,—
The love that comes of giving and of care.

Motherhood: Nursing with her heart-warm milk,
Fighting to death all danger to her young,
Hunting for food for little ones half-weaned,
Teaching them how to hunt and fight in turn,—
Then loving not till the new litter came.

Motherhood: When the little savage grew
Tall at his mother's side, and learned to feel
Some mother even in his father's heart,
Love coming to new babies while the first
Still needed mother's care, and therefore love,—
Love lasting longer because childhood did.

Motherhood: Semi-civilized, intense,
Fierce with brute passion, narrow with the range
Of slavish lives to meanest service bowed;
Devoted—to the sacrifice of life;
Jealous beyond belief, and ignorant
Even of what should keep the child alive.
Love spreading with the spread of human needs,
The child's new, changing, ever-growing wants,
Yet seeking like brute mothers of the past
To give all things to her own child herself.
Loving to the exclusion of all else;
To the child's service bending a whole life;
Yet stunting the young creature day by day
With lack of Justice, Liberty, and Peace.

Motherhood: Civilized. There stands at last,
Facing the heavens with as calm a smile,
The highest fruit of the long work of God;
The highest type of this, the highest race;
She from whose groping instinct grew all love—
All love—in which is all the life of man.

Motherhood: Seeing with her clear, kind eyes,
Luminous, tender eyes, wherein the smile
Is like the smile of sunlight on the sea,
That the new children of the newer day
Need more than any single heart can give,
More than is known to any single mind,
More than is found in any single house,
And need it from the day they see the light.
Then, measuring her love by what they need,
Gives, from the heart of modern motherhood.
Gives first, as tree to bear God's highest fruit,
A clean, strong body, perfect and full grown,
Fair for the purpose of its womanhood,
Not for light fancy of a lower mind;

Gives a clear mind, athletic, beautiful,
Dispassionate, unswerving from the truth;
Gives a great heart that throbs with human love,
As she would wish her son to love the world.

Then, when the child comes, lovely as a star,
She, in the peace of primal motherhood,
Nurses her baby with unceasing joy,
With milk of human kindness,[3] human health,
Bright human beauty, and immortal love.
And then? Ah! here is the New Motherhood—
The motherhood of the fair new-made world—
O glorious New Mother of New Men!
Her child, with other children from its birth,
In the unstinted freedom of warm air,
Under the wisest eyes, the tenderest thought,
Surrounded by all beauty and all peace,
Led, playing, through the gardens of the world,
With the crowned heads of science and great love
Mapping safe paths for those small, rosy feet,—
Taught human love by feeling human love,
Taught justice by the laws that rule his days,
Taught wisdom by the way in which he lives,
Taught to love all mankind and serve them fair
By seeing, from his birth, all children served
With the same righteous, all-embracing care.

O Mother! Noble Mother, yet to come!
How shall thy child point to the bright career
Of her of whom he boasts to be the son—
Not for assiduous service spent on him,
But for the wisdom which has set him forth
A clear-brained, pure-souled, noble-hearted man,
With health and strength and beauty his by birth;
And, more, for the wide record of her life,
Great work, well done, that makes him praise her name
And long to make as great a one his own!
And how shall all the children of the world,
Feeling all mothers love them, loving all,
Rise up and call her blessed!
      This shall be.


## Six Hours a Day

Six hours a day the woman spends on food!
Six mortal hours a day.. . . .
With fire and water toiling, heat and cold;
Struggling with laws she does not understand

Of chemistry and physics, and the weight
Of poverty and ignorance besides.
Toiling for those she loves, the added strain
Of tense-emotion on her humble skill,
The sensitiveness born of love and fear,
Making it harder to do even work.
Toiling without release, no hope ahead
Of taking up another business soon,
Of varying the task she finds too hard—
This, her career, so closely interknit
With holier demands as deep as life
That to refuse to cook is held the same
As to refuse her wife and motherhood.
Six mortal hours a day to handle food,—
Prepare it, serve it, clean it all away,—
With allied labors of the stove and tub,
The pan, the dishcloth, and the scrubbing-brush.
Developing forever in her brain
The power to do this work in which she lives;
While the slow finger of Heredity
Writes on the forehead of each living man,
Strive as he may, "His mother was a cook!"

## An Old Proverb

"As much pity to see a woman weep as to see a goose go barefoot."[4]

No escape, little creature! The earth hath no place
For the woman who seeketh to fly from her race.
Poor, ignorant, timid, too helpless to roam,
The woman must bear what befalls her, at home.
Bear bravely, bear dumbly—it is but the same
That all others endure who live under the name.
    No escape, little creature!

No escape under heaven! Can man treat you worse
After God has laid on you his infinite curse?[5]
The heaviest burden of sorrow you win
Cannot weigh with the load of original sin;
No shame be too black for the cowering face
Of her who brought shame to the whole human race!
    No escape under heaven!

Yet you feel, being human. You shrink from the pain
That each child, born a woman, must suffer again.
From the strongest of bonds heart can feel, man can shape,
You cannot rebel, or appeal, or escape.
You must bear and endure. If the heart cannot sleep,

And the pain groweth bitter,—too bitter,—then weep!
  For you feel, being human.

And she wept, being woman. The numberless years
Have counted her burdens and counted her tears;
The maid wept forsaken, the mother forlorn
For the child that was dead, and the child that was born.
Wept for joy—as a miracle!—wept in her pain!
Wept aloud, wept in secret, wept ever in vain!
  Still she weeps, being woman.

## Reassurance

Can you imagine nothing better, brother,
Than that which you have always had before?
Have you been so content with "wife and mother,"
  You dare hope nothing more?

Have you forever prized her, praised her, sung her,
The happy queen of a most happy reign?
Never dishonored her, despised her, flung her
  Derision and disdain?

Go ask the literature of all the ages!
Books that were written before women read!
Pagan and Christian, satirists and sages,—
  Read what the world has said!

There was no power on earth to bid you slacken
The generous hand that painted her disgrace!
There was no shame on earth too black to blacken
  That much-praised woman-face.

Eve[6] and Pandora![7]—always you begin it—
The ancients called her Sin and Shame and Death!
"There is no evil without woman in it,"
  The modern proverb saith!

She has been yours in uttermost possession,—
Your slave, your mother, your well-chosen bride,—
And you have owned, in million-fold confession,
  You were not satisfied.

Peace then! Fear not the coming woman, brother!
Owning herself, she giveth all the more!
She shall be better woman, wife and mother,
  Than man hath known before!

## Mother to Child

How best can I serve thee, my child! My child!
Flesh of my flesh and dear heart of my heart!

Once thou wast within me—I held thee—I fed thee—
By the force of my loving and longing I led thee—
    Now we are apart!

I may blind thee with kisses and crush with embracing,
Thy warm mouth in my neck and our arms interlacing;
But here in my body my soul lives alone,
And thou answerest me from a house of thine own,—
    That house which I builded!

Which we builded together, thy father and I;
In which thou must live, O my darling, and die!
Not one stone can I alter, one atom relay,—
Not to save or defend thee or help thee to stay—
    That gift is completed!

How best can I serve thee? O child, if they knew
How my heart aches with loving! How deep and how true,
How brave and enduring, how patient, how strong,
How longing for good and how fearful of wrong,
    Is the love of thy mother!

Could I crown thee with riches! Surround, overflow thee
With fame and with power till the whole world should know thee;
With wisdom and genius to hold the world still,
To bring laughter and tears, joy and pain, at thy will,
    Still—*thou* mightst not be happy!

Such have lived—and in sorrow. The greater the mind
The wider and deeper the grief it can find.
The richer, the gladder, the more thou canst feel
The keen stings that a lifetime is sure to reveal.
    O my child! Must thou suffer?

Is there no way my life can save thine from a pain?
Is the love of a mother no possible gain?
No labor of Hercules[8]—search for the Grail[9]—
No way for this wonderful love to avail?
    God in Heaven—O teach me!

My prayer has been answered. The pain thou must bear
Is the pain of the world's life which thy life must share.
Thou art one with the world—though I love thee the best;
And to save thee from pain I must save all the rest—
    Well—with God's help I'll do it!

Thou art one with the rest. I must love thee in them.
Thou wilt sin with the rest; and thy mother must stem
The world's sin. Thou wilt weep; and thy mother must dry
The tears of the world lest her darling should cry.
    I will do it—God helping!

And I stand not alone. I will gather a band
Of all loving mothers from land unto land.
Our children are part of the world! do ye hear?
They are one with the world—we must hold them all dear!
    Love all for the child's sake!

For the sake of my child I must hasten to save
All the children on earth from the jail and the grave.
For so, and so only, I lighten the share
Of the pain of the world that my darling must bear—
    Even so, and so only!


## Services

She was dead. Forth went the word,
And every creature heard.
To the last hamlet in the farthest lands,
To people countless as the sands
Of primal seas.

And with the word so sent
Her life's full record went,—
Of what fair line, how gifted, how endowed,
How educated; and then, told aloud,
The splendid tale of what her life had done;
And all the people heard and felt as one;
Exulting all together in their dead,
And the grand story of the life she led.

But in the city where her body lay
Great services were held on that fair day:
People by thousands; music to the sky;
Flowers of a garnered season; winding by,
Processions, glorious in rich array,
All massing in the temple where she lay.

Then, when the music rested, rose and stood
Those who could speak of her and count the good,
The measureless great good her life had spread,
That all might hear the praises of their dead.
And those who loved her sent from the world's end
Their tribute to the memory of their friend;
While teachers to their children whispered low,
"See that you have as many when you go!"

Then was recited how her life had part
In building up this science and that arInventing here, administering there,
Helping to organize, create, prepare,
With fullest figures to expatiate

On her unmeasured value to the state.
And the child, listening, grew in noble pride,
And planned for greater praises when he died.

Then the Poet spoke of those long ripening years;
And tenderer music brought the grateful tears;
And then, lest grief upon their heartstrings hang,
Her children stood around the bier and sang:

> In the name of the mother that bore us—
> > Bore us strong—bore us free—
> We will strive in the labors before us,
> > Even as she! Even as she!

> In the name of her wisdom and beauty,
> > Of her life full of light,
> We will live in our national duty,
> > We will help on the right:

> We will love as her heart loved before us,
> > Warm and wide—strong and high!
> In the name of the mother that bore us,
> > We will live! We will die!

## In Mother-Time

When woman looks at woman with the glory in her eyes,
When eternity lies open like a scroll,
When immortal life is being felt,—the life that never dies,—
> And the triumph of it ringeth
> And the sweetness of it singeth
> > In the soul,

Then we come to California, the Garden of the Lord,
Through all its leagues of endless blossoming;
And we sing, we sing together, to the whole world's deep accord—
> And we feel each other praying
> Over what the flowers are saying
> > As we sing.

We were waiting, we were growing, glad of heart and strong of soul,
Like the peace and power of all these virgin lands;
Through the years of holy maidenhood with motherhood for goal—
> And soon we shall be holding
> Fruit of all life's glad unfolding
> > In our hands.

White-robed mothers, flower-crowned mothers, in the splendor of their youth,
In the grandeur of maturity and power;
Feeling life has passed the telling in its joyousness and truth,

Feeling life will soon be giving
Them the golden key of living
    In one hour.

We come to California for the sunshine and the flowers;
Our motherhood has brought us here as one;
For the fruit of all the ages should share the shining hours,
    With the blossoms ever-springing
    And the golden globes low swinging,
        In the sun.


## She Who is to Come

A woman—in so far as she beholdeth
    Her one Beloved's face;
A mother—with a great heart that enfoldeth
    The children of the Race;
A body, free and strong, with that high beauty
    That comes of perfect use, is built thereof;
A mind where Reason ruleth over Duty,
    And Justice reigns with Love;
A self-poised, royal soul, brave, wise and tender,
    No longer blind and dumb;
A Human Being, of an unknown splendor,
    Is she who is to come!


## Girls of To-day

    Girls of to-day! Give ear!
Never since time began
Has come to the race of man
A year, a day, an hour,
So full of promise and power
    As the time that now is here!

    Never in all the lands
Was there a power so great,
To move the wheels of state,
To lift up body and mind,
To waken the deaf and blind,
    As the power that is in your hands!

    Here at the gates of gold
You stand in the pride of youth,
Strong in courage and truth,
Stirred by a force kept back
Through centuries long and black,
    Armed with a power threefold!

First: You are makers of men!
Then Be the things you preach!
Let your own greatness teach!
When mothers like this you see
Men will be strong and free—
        Then, and not till then!

        Second: Since Adam fell,
Have you not heard it said
That men by women are led?
True is the saying—true!
See to it what you do!
        See that you lead them well.

        Third: You have work of your own!
Maid and mother and wife,
Look in the face of life!
There are duties you owe the race!
Outside your dwelling-place
        There is work for you alone!

        Maid and mother and wife,
See your own work be done!
Be worthy a noble son!
Help man in the upward way!
Truly, a girl to-day
        Is the strongest thing in life!


## "We, as Women"

There's a cry in the air about us—
        We hear it, before, behind—
Of the way in which "we, as women,"
        Are going to lift mankind!

With our white frocks starched and ruffled,
        And our soft hair brushed and curled—
Hats off! for "We, as women,"
        Are coming to save the world.

Fair sisters! listen one moment—
        And perhaps you'll pause for ten:
The business of women as women
        Is only with men as men!

What we do, "we, as women,"
        We have done all through our life;
The work that is ours as women
        Is the work of mother and wife!

But to elevate public opinion,
    And to lift up erring man,
Is the work of the Human Being;
    Let us do it—if we can.

But wait, warm-hearted sisters—
    Not quite so fast, so far.
Tell me how we are going to lift a thing
    Any higher than we are!

We are going to "purify politics,"
    And to "elevate the press."
We enter the foul paths of the world
    To sweeten and cleanse and bless.

To hear the high things we are going to do,
    And the horrors of man we tell,
One would think, "we, as women," were angels,
    And our brothers were fiends of hell.

We, that were born of one mother,
    And reared in the selfsame place,
In the school and the church together,—
    We of one blood, one race!

Now then, all forward together!
    But remember, every one,
That it is not by feminine innocence
    The work of the world is done.

The world needs strength and courage,
    And wisdom to help and feed—
When, "we, as women" bring these to man,
    We shall lift the world indeed.


## If Mother Knew

If mother knew the way I felt,—
    And I'm sure a mother should,—
She wouldn't make it quite so hard
    For a person to be good!

I want to do the way she says;
    I try to all day long;
And then she just skips all the right,
    And pounces on the wrong!

A dozen times I do a thing,
    And one time I forget;
And then she looks at me and asks
    If I can't remember yet?

She'll tell me to do something,
    And I'll really start to go;
But she'll keep right on telling it
    As if I didn't know.

Till it seems as if I couldn't—
    It makes me kind of wild;
And then she says she never saw
    Such a disobliging child.

I go to bed all sorry,
    And say my prayers, and cry,
And mean next day to be so good
    I just can't wait to try.

And I get up next morning,
    And mean to do just right;
But mother's sure to scold me
    About something, before night.

I wonder if she really thinks
    A child could go so far,
As to be perfect all the time
    As the grown up people are!

If she only knew I tried to,—
    And I'm sure a mother should,—
She wouldn't make it quite so hard
    For a person to be good!

## The Anti-Suffragists

Fashionable women in luxurious homes,
With men to feed them, clothe them, pay their bills,
Bow, doff the hat, and fetch the handkerchief;
Hostess or guest; and always so supplied
With graceful deference and courtesy;
Surrounded by their horses, servants, dogs,—
These tell us they have all the rights they want.

Successful women who have won their way
Alone, with strength of their unaided arm,
Or helped by friends, or softly climbing up
By the sweet aid of "woman's influence";
Successful any way, and caring naught
For any other woman's unsuccess,—
These tell us they have all the rights they want.

Religious women of the feebler sort,—
Not the religion of a righteous world,

A free, enlightened, upward-reaching world,
But the religion that considers life
As something to back out of!—whose ideal
Is to renounce, submit, and sacrifice.
Counting on being patted on the head
And given a high chair when they get to heaven,—
These tell us they have all the rights they want.

Ignorant women—college-bred sometimes,
But ignorant of life's realities
And principles of righteous government,
And how the privileges they enjoy
Were won with blood and tears by those before—
Those they condemn, whose ways they now oppose;
Saying, "Why not let well enough alone?"
Our world is very pleasant as it is,"—
These tell us they have all the rights they want.

And selfish women,—pigs in petticoats,—
Rich, poor, wise, unwise, top or bottom round,
But all sublimely innocent of thought,
And guiltless of ambition, save the one
Deep, voiceless aspiration—to be fed!
These have no use for rights or duties more.
Duties today are more than they can meet,
And law insures their right to clothes and food,—
These tell us they have all the rights they want.

And, more's the pity, some good women, too;
Good, conscientious women with ideas;
Who think—or think they think—that woman's cause
Is best advanced by letting it alone;
That she somehow is not a human thing,
And not to be helped on by human means,
Just added to humanity—an "L"[10]—
A wing, a branch, an extra, not mankind,—
These tell us they have all the rights they want.

And out of these has come a monstrous thing,
A strange, down-sucking whirlpool of disgrace,
Women uniting against womanhood,
And using that great name to hide their sin!
Vain are their words as that old king's command
Who set his will against the rising tide.
But who shall measure the historic shame
Of these poor traitors—traitors are they all—
To great Democracy and Womanhood!

## Women Do Not Want It

When the woman suffrage argument first stood upon its legs,
They answered it with cabbages, they answered it with eggs,
They answered it with ridicule, they answered it with scorn,
They thought it a monstrosity that should not have been born.

When the woman suffrage argument grew vigorous and wise,
And was not to be answered by these apposite replies,
They turned their opposition into reasoning severe
Upon the limitations of our God-appointed sphere.

We were told of disabilities,—a long array of these,
Till one could think that womanhood was merely a disease;
And "the maternal sacrifice" was added to the plan
Of the various sacrifices we have always made—to man.

Religionists and scientists, in amity and bliss,
However else they disagreed, could all agree on this,
And the gist of all their discourse, when you got down in it,
Was—we could not have the ballot because we were not fit!

They would not hear the reason, they would not fairly yield,
They would not own their arguments were beaten in the field;
But time passed on, and someway, we need not ask them how,
Whatever ails those arguments—we do not hear them now!

You may talk of suffrage now with an educated man,
And he agrees with all you say, as sweetly as he can;
'Twould be better for us all, of course, if womanhood was free;
But "the women do not want it"—and so it must not be!

'Tis such a tender thoughtfulness! So exquisite a care!
Not to pile on our frail shoulders what we do not wish to bear!
But, oh, most generous brother! Let us look a little more—
Have we women always wanted what you gave to us before?

Did we ask for veils and harems in the Oriental races?
Did we beseech to be "unclean," shut out of sacred places?
Did we beg for scolding bridles[11] and ducking stools[12] to come?
And clamor for the beating stick no thicker than your thumb?

Did we ask to be forbidden from all the trades that pay?
Did we claim the lower wages for a man's full work to-day?
Have we petitioned for the laws wherein our shame is shown:
That not a woman's child—nor her own body—is her own?

What women want has never been a strongly acting cause,
When woman has been wronged by man in churches, customs, laws;
Why should he find this preference so largely in his way
When he himself admits the right of what we ask to-day?

## Wedded Bliss[13]

"O come and be my mate!" said the Eagle to the Hen,
    "I love to soar, but then
    I want my mate to rest
    Forever in the nest!"
    Said the Hen, "I cannot fly,
    I have no wish to try,
But I joy to see my mate careening through the sky!"
They wed, and cried, "Ah, this is Love, my own!"
And the Hen sat, the Eagle soared, alone.

"O come and be my mate!" said the Lion to the Sheep;
    "My love for you is deep!
    I slay, a Lion should,
    But you are mild and good!"
    Said the sheep, "I do no ill—
    Could not, had I the will—
But I joy to see my mate pursue, devour and kill."
They wed, and cried, "Ah, this is Love, my own!"
And the Sheep browsed, the Lion prowled, alone.

"O come and be my mate!" said the Salmon to the Clam;
    "You are not wise, but I am.
    I know sea and stream as well;
    You know nothing but your shell."
    Said the Clam, "I'm slow of motion,
    But my love is all devotion,
And I joy to have my mate traverse lake and stream and ocean!"
They wed, and cried, "Ah, this is Love, my own!"
And the Clam sucked, the Salmon swam, alone.


## The Holy Stove

O the soap-vat is a common thing!
    The pickle-tub is low!
The loom and wheel have lost their grace
In falling from the dwelling-place
    To mills where all may go!
The bread-tray needeth not your love;
    The wash-tub wide doth roam;
Even the oven free may rove;
But bow ye down to the Holy Stove,
    The Altar of the Home!

Before it bend the worshippers,
    And wreaths of parsley twine;
Above it still the incense curls,
And a passing train of hired girls

Do service at the shrine.
We toil to keep the altar crowned
　　With dishes new and nice,
And Art and Love, and Time and Truth,
We offer up, with Health and Youth,
　　In daily sacrifice.

Speak not to us of a fairer faith,
　　Of a lifetime free from pain.
Our fathers always worshipped here,
Our mothers served this altar drear,
　　And still we serve amain.
Our earliest dreams around it cling,
　　Bright hopes that childhood sees,
And memory leaves a vista wide
Where Mother's Doughnuts[14] rank beside
　　The thought of Mother's Knees.[15]

The wood-box hath no sanctity;
　　No glamour gilds the coal;
But the Cook-Stove is a sacred thing
To which a reverent faith we bring
　　And serve with heart and soul.
The Home's a temple all divine,
　　By the Poker and the Hod![16]
The Holy Stove is the altar fine,
The wife the priestess at the shrine—
　　Now who can be the god?

## The Mother's Charge

She raised her head. With hot and glittering eye,
"I know," she said, "that I am going to die.
Come here, my daughter, while my mind is clear.
Let me make plain to you your duty here;
My duty once—I never failed to try—
But for some reason I am going to die."
She raised her head, and, while her eyes rolled wild,
Poured these instructions on the gasping child:

"Begin at once—don't iron sitting down—
Wash your potatoes when the fat is brown—
Monday, unless it rains—it always pays
To get fall sewing done on the right days—
A carpet-sweeper and a little broom—
Save dishes—wash the summer dining-room
With soda—keep the children out of doors—
The starch is out—beeswax on all the floors—

If girls are treated like your friends they stay—
They stay, and treat you like their friends—the way
To make home happy is to keep a jar—
And save the prettiest pieces for the star
In the middle—blue's too dark—all silk is best—
And don't forget the corners—when they're dressed
Put them on ice—and always wash the chest
Three times a day, the windows every week—
We need more flour—the bedroom ceilings leak—
It's better than onion—keep the boys at home—
Gardening is good—a load, three loads of loam—
They bloom in spring—and smile, smile always, dear—
Be brave, keep on—I hope I've made it clear."

She died as all her mothers died before.
Her daughter died in turn, and made one more.


## A Brood Mare

It is a significant fact that the phenomenal improvement in horses during recent years is accompanied by the growing conviction that good points and a good record are as desirable in the dam as in the sire, if not more so.[17]

I had a quarrel yesterday,
    A violent dispute,
With a man who tried to sell to me
    A strange amorphous brute;

A creature disproportionate,
    A beast to make you stare,
An undeveloped, overgrown,
    Outrageous-looking mare.

Her fore legs they were weak and thin,
    Her hind legs weak and fat;
She was heavy in the quarters,
    With a narrow chest and flat;

And she had managed to combine—
    I'm sure I don't know how—
The barrel of a greyhound
    With the belly of a cow.

She seemed exceeding feeble,
    And he owned with manner bland
That she walked a little, easily,
    But wasn't fit to stand.

I tried to mount the animal
    To test her on the track;

But he cried in real anxiety,
  "Get off! You'll strain her back!"

And then I sought to harness her,
  But he explained at length
That any draught or carriage work
  Was quite beyond her strength.

"No use to carry or to pull!
  No use upon the course!"
Said I, "How can you have the face
  To call that thing a horse?"

Said he, indignantly, "I don't!
  I'm dealing on the square;
I never said it was a horse,
  I told you 'twas a mare!

"A mare was never meant to race,
  To carry, or to pull;
She is meant for breeding only, so
  Her place in life is full."

Said I, "Do you pretend to breed
  From such a beast as that?
A mass of shapeless skin and bone,
  Or shapeless skin and fat?"

Said he, "Her sire was thoroughbred,
  As fine as walked the earth,
And all her colts receive from him
  The marks of noble birth;

"And then I mate her carefully
  With horses fine and fit;
Mares do not need to have themselves
  The points which they transmit!"

Said I, "Do you pretend to say
  You can raise colts as fair
From that fat cripple as you can
  From an able-bodied mare?"

Quoth he, "I solemnly assert,
  Just as I said before,
A mare that's good for breeding
  Can be good for nothing more!"

Cried I, "One thing is certain proof;
  One thing I want to see;
Trot out the noble colts you raise
  From your anomaly."

He looked a little dashed at this,
     And the poor mare hung her head.
"Fact is," said he, "she's had but one,
     And that one—well, it's dead!"


## Feminine Vanity

Feminine Vanity! O ye Gods! Hear to this man!
     As if silk and velvet and feathers and fur
     And jewels and gold had been just for her,
          Since the world began!

Where is his memory? Let him look back—all of the way!
     Let him study the history of his race
     From the first he-savage that painted his face
          To the dude of to-day!

Vanity! Oh! Are the twists and curls The intricate patterns in red, black, and blue,
     The wearisome tortures of rich tattoo,
          Just made for girls?

Is it only the squaw who files the teeth,
     And dangles the lip, and bores the ear,
     And wears bracelet and necklet and anklet as queer
          As the bones beneath?

Look at the soldier, the noble, the king!
     Egypt or Greece or Rome discloses
     The purples and perfumes and gems and roses
          On a masculine thing!

Look at the men of our own dark ages!
     Heroes too, in their cloth of gold,
     With jewels as thick as the cloth could hold,
          On the knights and pages!

We wear false hair? Our man looks big!
     But it's not so long, let me beg to state,
     Since every gentleman shaved his pate
          And wore a wig.

French heels?[18] Sharp toes? See our feet defaced?
     But there was a day when the soldier free
     Tied the toe of his shoe to the manly knee—
          Yes, and even his waist!

We pad and stuff? Our man looks bolder.
     Don't speak of the time when a bran-filled bunch
     Made an English gentleman look like Punch[19]—
          But feel of his shoulder!

Feminine Vanity! O ye Gods! Hear to these men!
 Vanity's wide as the world is wide!
 Look at the peacock in his pride—
  Is it a hen?

## The Modest Maid

I am a modest San Francisco maid,
 Fresh, fair, and young,
Such as the painter gladly have displayed,
 The poets sing.

Modest?—Oh, modest as a bud unblown,
 A thought unspoken;
Hidden and cherished, unbeheld, unknown,
 In peace unbroken.

Far from the holy shades of this my home,
 The coarse world raves,
And the New Woman[20] cries to heaven's dome
 For what she craves.

Loud, vulgar, public, screaming from the stage,
 Her skirt divided.[21]
Riding cross-saddled on the dying age,
 Justly derided.

I blush for her, I blush for our sweet sex
 By her disgraced.
My sphere is home. My soul I do not vex
 With zeal misplaced.

Come then to me with happy heart, O man!
 I wait your visit.
To guide your footsteps I do all I can,
 Am most explicit.

As veined flower-petals teach the passing bee
 The way to honey,
So printer's ink displayed instructeth thee
 Where lies my money.

Go see! In type and cut across the page,
 Before the nation,
There you may read about my eyes, my age,
 My education.

My fluffy golden hair, my tiny feet
 My pet ambition,
My well-developed figure, and my sweet,
 Retiring disposition.

All, all is there, and now I coyly wait.
  Pray don't delay.
My address does the Blue Book[22] plainly state,
  And mamma's "day."[23]


## Unsexed

It was a wild rebellious drone
  That loudly did complain;
He wished he was a worker bee[24]
  With all his might and main.

"I want to work," the drone declared.
  Quoth they, "The thing you mean
Is that you scorn to be a drone
  And long to be a queen.

"You long to lay unnumbered eggs,
  And rule the waiting throng;
You long to lead our summer flight,
  And this is rankly wrong."

Cried he, "My life is pitiful!
  I only eat and wed,
And in my marriage is the end—
  Thereafter I am dead.

"I would I were the busy bee
  That flits from flower to flower;
I long to share in work and care
  And feel the worker's power."

Quoth they, "The life you dare to spurn
  Is set before you here
As your one great, prescribed, ordained,
  Divinely ordered sphere!

"Without your services as drone,
  We should not be alive;
Your modest task, when well fulfilled,
  Preserves the busy hive.

"Why underrate your blessed power?
  Why leave your rightful throne
To choose a field of life that's made
  For working bees alone?"

Cried he, "But it is not enough,
  My momentary task!
Let me do that and more beside:
  To work is all I ask!"

Then fiercely rose the workers all,
    For sorely were they vexed;
"O wretch!" they cried, "should this betide,
    You would become unsexed!"

And yet he had not sighed for eggs,
    Nor yet for royal mien;
He longed to be a worker bee,
    But not to be a queen.

## Females

The female fox she is a fox;
    The female whale a whale;
The female eagle holds her place
As representative of race
    As truly as the male.

The mother hen doth scratch for her chicks,
    And scratch for herself beside;
The mother cow doth nurse her calf,
Yet fares as well as her other half
    In the pasture far and wide.

The female bird doth soar in air;
    The female fish doth swim;
The fleet-foot mare upon the course
Doth hold her own with the flying horse—
    Yea, and she beateth him!

One female in the world we find
    Telling a different tale.
It is the female of our race,
Who holds a parasitic place
    Dependent on the male.

Not so, saith she, ye slander me!
    No parasite am I!
I earn my living as a wife;
My children take my very life.
Why should I share in human strife.
    To plant and build and buy?

The human race holds highest place
    In all the world so wide,
Yet these inferior females wive,
And raise their little ones alive,
And feed themselves beside.

The race is higher than the sex,
    Though sex be fair and good;

A Human Creature is your state,
And to be human is more great
    Than even womanhood!

The female fox she is a fox;
    The female whale a whale;
The female eagle holds her place
As representative of race
    As truly as the male.

## A Mother's Soliloquy

You soft, pink, moving thing!
Young limbs that crave
Motion as free as zephyr-lifted wave;
Uneasy with the push of unlearned powers!
Exploring slowly through half-conscious hours;
With what rich new surprise and joy you feel
Your own will move yourself from head to heel!
So, let me swaddle you in bandage tight,
Dress you in wide, confining folds of white,
Cover you warmly, hold you close, and so
A mother's instinct-guided love I'll show!

Mysterious little frame!
Each organ new
And learning swiftly what it has to do!
Thy life's bright stream—as yet so newly thing—
Refreshed by heaven's sunlit air divine;
With what delight you breathe in rosy ease
The strengthening, restful, blossom-scented breeze!
So, let me wrap you in a blanket shawl,
And veil your face in woolen, when at all
You meet the air. Here in my arms is best
The curtained bedroom where your elders rest;
So shall I guard you from a draught, and so
A mother's instinct-guided love I'll show.

Young earnest mind at work!
Each sense attends
To teach you life's approaching foes and friends;
Eye, ear, nose, tongue, and ever ready hand,
Eager to help you learn and understand.
What floods of happiness the day insures,
While each new knowledge is becoming yours!
So, let me firmly take away from you
The things you so persistently would view;
And when you stretch the hand that tells so much,

Rap your soft knuckles and exclaim, "Don't touch!"
I'll tell you what you ought to learn, and so,
A mother's instinct-guided love I'll show.

An ordinary child at best,
So neighbors tell;
Not very large and strong, not very well;
A victim to the measles and the croup,
Fevers that flush and chill, and coughs that whoop;
To unknown naughtiness and well-known pain;
No racial progress[25] here—no special gain!
But I, your mother, see with other eyes;
I hold you second to none under skies,
This estimate, unbased on any fact,
Shall teach you how to feel and how to act,
Shall make you wise, and true, and strong, and so,
A mother's instinct-guided love I'll show.


## They Wandered Forth

They wandered forth in springtime woods,
    Three women, thickly hung
With yards and yards of woollen goods—
    To play that they were young!

The river raced with the racing air;
    The woods were wild with song;
The glad birds darted everywhere—
    And so they walked along!

Stiff-bodied, fat, oppressed with cloth,
    Dull-colored, sad to see,
Slow-moving over the bright grass,
Their shapeless shadows fall and pass,
And dreaming not—alas! alas!
    Of what dear light might be!


## Baby Love

Baby Love came prancing by,
Cap on head and sword on thigh,
Horse to ride and drum to beat,—
All the world beneath his feet.

Mother Life was sitting there,
Hard at work and full of care,
Set of mouth and sad of eye.
Baby Love came prancing by.

Baby Love was very proud,
Very lively, very loud;
Mother Life arose in wrath,
Set an arm across his path.

Baby Love wept loud and long,
But his mother's arm was strong.
Mother had to work, she said.
Baby Love was put to bed.

# THE MARCH

## The Wolf at the Door[1]

There's a haunting horror near us
    That nothing drives away:
Fierce lamping eyes at nightfall,
    A crouching shade by day;
There's a whining at the threshold,
    There's a scratching at the floor.
To work! To work! In Heaven's name!
    The wolf is at the door!

The day was long, the night was short,
    The bed was hard and cold;
Still weary are the little ones,
    Still weary are the old.
We are weary in our cradles
    From our mother's toil untold;
We are born to hoarded weariness
    As some to hoarded gold.

We will not rise! We will not work!
    Nothing the day can give
Is half so sweet as an hour of sleep;
    Better to sleep than live!
What power can stir these heavy limbs?
    What hope these dull hearts swell?
What fear more cold, what pain more sharp,
    Than the life we know so well?

To die like a man by lead or steel
    Is nothing that we should fear;
No human death would be worse to feel
    Than the life that holds us here.
But this is a fear no heart can face—
    A fate no man can dare—
To be run to earth and die by the teeth
    Of the gnawing monster there!

The slow, relentless, padding step
    That never goes astray—
The rustle in the underbrush—
    The shadow in the way—
The straining light—the long pursuit—
    The steady gain behind—
Death-wearied man and tireless brute,
    And the struggle wild and blind!

There's a hot breath at the keyhole
    And a tearing as of teeth!
Well do I know the bloodshot eyes

And the dripping jaws beneath!
There's a whining at the threshold—
    There's a scratching at the floor—
To work! To work! In Heaven's name!
    The wolf is at the door!

## The Lost Game

Came the big children to the little ones,
    And unto them full pleasantly did say,
"Lo! we have spread for you a merry game,
And ye shall all be winners at the same.
    Come now and play!"

    *Great is the game they enter in,—*
        *Rouge et Noir[2] on a giant scale,—*
    *Red with blood and black with sin,*
    *Where many must lose and few may win,*
        *And the players never fail!*

Said the strong children to the weaker ones,
    "See, ye are many, and we are but few!
The mass of all the counters ye divide,
But few remain to share upon our side.
    Play—as we do!"

    *Strange is the game they enter in,—*
        *Rouge et Noir on a field of pain!*
    *And the silver white and the yellow gold*
    *Pile and pile in the victor's hold,*
        *While the many play in vain!*

Said the weak children to the stronger ones,
    "See now, howe'er it fall, we lose our share!
And play we well or ill we always lose;
While ye gain always more than ye can use.
    Bethink ye—is it fair?"

    *Strange is the game they enter in,—*
        *Rouge et Noir, and the bank is strong!*
    *Play they well or play they wide*
    *The gold is still on the banker's side,*
        *And the game endureth long.*

Said the strong children, each aside to each,
    "The game is slow—our gains are all too small!"
Play we together now, 'gainst them apart;
So shall these dull ones lose it from the start,
    And we shall gain it all!"

*Strange is the game that now they win,—*
*Rouge et Noir with a new design!*
*What can the many players do*
*Whose wits are weak and counters few*
*When the Power and the Gold combine?*

Said the weak children to the stronger ones,
"We care not for the game!
For play as we may our chance is small,
And play as ye may ye have it all.
The end's the same!"

*Strange is the game the world doth play,—*
*Rouge et Noir, with the counters gold,*
*Red with blood and black with sin;*
*Few and fewer are they that win*
*As the ages pass untold.*

Said the strong children to the weaker ones,
"Ye lose in laziness! ye lose in sleep!
Play faster now and make the counters spin!
Play well, as we, and ye in time shall win!
Play fast! Play deep!"

*Strange is the game of Rouge et Noir,—*
*Never a point have the little ones won.*
*The winners are strong and flushed with gain,*
*The losers are weak with want and pain,*
*And still the game goes on.*

But those rich players grew so very few,
So many grew the poor ones, that one day
They rose up from that table, side by side,
Calm, countless, terrible—they rose and cried
In one great voice that shook the heavens wide,
"WE WILL NOT PLAY!"

*Where is the game of Rouge et Noir?*
*Where is the wealth of yesterday?*
*What availeth the power ye tell,*
*And the skill in the game ye play so well?*
*If the players will not play?*

## The Looker-On

The world was full of the battle,
The whole world far and wide;
Men and women and children
Were fighting on either side.

I was sent from the hottest combat
    With a message of life and death,
Black with smoke and red with blood,
    Weary and old of breath,

Forced to linger a moment,
    And bind a stubborn wound,
Cursing the hurt that kept me back
    From the fiery battle-ground.

When I found a cheerful stranger,
    Calm, critical, serene,
Well sheltered from all danger,
    Painting a battle-scene.

He was cordially glad to see me—
    The coolly smiling wretch—
And inquired with admiration,
    "Do you mind if I make a sketch?"

So he had me down in a minute,
    With murmurs of real delight;
My "color" was "delicious,"
    My "action" was "just right!"

And he prattled on with ardor
    Of the moving scene below;
Of the "values" of the smoke-wreaths,
    And "the splendid rush and go"

Of the headlong desperate charges
    Where a thousand lives were spent;
Of the "massing" in the foreground
    With the "middle distance" blent.

Said I, "You speak serenely
    Of the living death in view.
These are human creatures dying—
    Are you not human too?

"This is a present battle,
    Where all men strive to-day.
How does it chance you sit apart?
    Which is your banner—say!"

His fresh cheek blanched a little,
    But he answered with a smile
That he fought not on either side;
    He was watching a little while.

"Watching!" said I, "and neutral!
    Neutral in times like these!"

And I plucked him off his sketching stool
And brought him to his knees.

I stripped him of his travelling cloak
And showed him to the sky:
By his uniform—a traitor!
By his handiwork—a spy!

I dragged him back to the field he left;
To the fate he was fitted for.
We have no place for lookers on
When all the world's at war!

## The Old-Time Wail

An Associated Press dispatch describes the utterance of a Farmers' Alliance meeting
in Kansas as consisting mostly of "the old-time wail of distress."[3]

Still Dives hath no peace.[4] Broken his slumber,
His feasts are troubled, and his pleasures fail;
For still he hears from voices without number
The same old wail.

They gather yet in field and town and city,—
The people, discontented, bitter, pale,—
And murmur of oppression, pain, and pity,—
The old-time wail.

And weary Dives, jaded in his pleasures,
Finding the endless clamor tiresome, stale—
Would gladly give a part of his wide treasures
To quiet that old wail.

Old? Yes, as old as Egypt. Sounding lowly
From naked millions, in the desert hid,
Starving and bleeding while they builded, slowly,
The Pharaohs' pyramid.

As old as Rome. That endless empire's minions
Raised ever and again the same dull cry;
And even Cæsar's eagle bent his pinions
While it disturbed the sky.

As old as the Dark Ages. The lean peasant,
Numerous, patient, still as time went by
Made his lord's pastimes something less than pleasant
With that unceasing cry.

It grew in volume down the crowding ages;
Unheeded still, and unappeased, it swelled.
And now it pleads in vain, and now it rages—
The answer still withheld.

A century ago it shrieked and clamored
    Till trembled emperors and kings grew pale;
At gates of palaces it roared and hammered,—
      The same old wail.

It got no final answer, though its passion
    Altered the face of Europe, monarchs slew;
But ere it sank to silence, in some fashion
      Others were wailing, too.

And now in broad America we hear it,—
    From crowded street, from boundless hill and vale.
Hear, Dives! Have ye not some cause to fear it,—
      This old-time wail?

Louder, my brother! Let us wail no longer
    Like those past sufferers whose hearts did break.
We are a wiser race, a braver, stronger—
      Let us not ask, but take!

So Dives shall have no distress soever,
    No sound of anguished voice by land or sea;
The oldtime wail shall so be stilled forever,
      And Dives shall not be!

## Free Land is Not Enough

Free land is not enough. In earliest days
When man, the baby, from the earth's bare breast
Drew for himself his simple sustenance,
Then freedom and his effort were enough.
The world to which a man is born to-day
Is a constructed, human, man-built world.
As the first savage needed the free wood,
We need the road, the ship, the bridge, the house,
The government, society, and church,—
These are the basis of our life to-day,
As much necessities to modern man
As was the forest to his ancestor.
To say to the new-born, "Take here your land;
In primal freedom settle where you will,
And work your own salvation in the world,"
Is but to put the last come upon earth
Back with the dim forerunners of his race
To climb the race's stairway in one life!
Allied society owes to the young—
The new men come to carry on the world—
Account for all the past, the deeds, the keys,
Full access to the riches of the earth.

Why? That these new ones may not be compelled,
Each for himself, to do our work again—
But reach their manhood even with to-day,
And gain to-morrow sooner. To go on—
To start from where we are and go ahead—
That is true progress, true humanity!

## Who is to Blame?

Who was to blame in that old time
    Of the unnoticed groan,
When prisoners without proof of crime
Rotted in dungeons wet with slime,
    And died unknown?

When torture was a common thing,
    When fire could speak,
When the flayed wretch hung quivering,
And rack-strained tendons, string by string,
    Snapped with a shriek?

Is it the Headsman, following still
    The laws his masters give?
Is it the Church or King who kill?
Or just the People, by whose will
    Church, King, and Headsman live?

The People, bowing slavish knee
    With tribute fruits of earth;
The People, gathering to see
The stake, the axe, the gallows-tree,
    In brutal mirth!

The People, countenancing pain
    By willing presence there;
The People—you might shriek in vain,
Poor son of Abel or of Cain[5]—
    The People did not care!

And now, in this fair age we're in,
    Who is to blame?
When men go mad and women sin
Because the life they struggle in
    Enforces shame!

When torture is so deep, so wide—
    The kind we give—
So long drawn out, so well supplied,
That men die now by suicide,
    Rather than live!

Is it the Rich Man, grinding still
     The faces of the Poor?
Is it our System which must kill?
Or just the People, by whose will
     That system can endure?

The People, bowing slavish knee
     With tribute fruits of earth;
The People, who can bear to see
In crime and death and poverty
     Fair ground for mirth!

The People, countenancing pain
     By willing presence there;
The People—you may shriek in vain—
Protest, rebel, beseech, complain—
     The People do not care!

Each man and woman feels the weight
     Of their own private share;
But for the suffering of the state,
That falls on all men soon or late,
     The People do not care!


## If a Man May Not Eat Neither Can He Work[6]

How can he work? He never has been taught
     The free use of what faculties he had.
Why should he work? Who ever yet has thought
     To give a love of working to the lad.

How can he work? His life has felt the lack
     Of all that makes us work; the proud, the free,
Each saying to the world, "I give you back
     Part of the glory you have given me!"

Why should he work? He has no honor high,
     Born of great trust and wealth and sense of power;
Honor, that makes us yearn before we die
     To add our labor to the world's rich dower.

How can he work? He has no inner strength
     Urging him on to action, no desire
To strain and wrestle, to achieve at length,
     Burning in all his veins,—a hidden fire.

Why should he work? There is no debt behind
     That man's nobility most longs to pay;
No claim upon him,—only the one blind
     Brute instinct that his dinner lies that way.

And that is not enough. Who may not eat
    Freely at life's full table all his youth,
Can never work in power and joy complete,
    In fullness, and in honor, and in truth.

## His Own Labor

Let every man be given what he earns!
We cry, and call it justice. Let him have
The product of his labor—and no more!
Well, then, let us begin with life's first needs,
And give him of the earth what he can make;
As much of air and light as he can make,
As much of ocean, and sweet wind and rain,
And flowers, and grass, and fruit, as he can make.
But no, we answer this is mockery:
No man makes these things. But of human wealth
Let every man be given what he makes,
The product of his labor, and no more.
Ah, well! So to the farmer let us give
Corn, and still corn, and only corn at last.
So to the grazier, meat; the fisher, fish;
Cloth to the weaver; to the mason, walls;
And let the writer sit and read his books—
The product of his labor—and naught else!
But no, we answer! Still you laugh at us.
We mean not his own labor in that sense,
But his share in the work of other men.
As much of what they make as he can buy
In fair exchange for labor of his own.
So let it be. As much of life's rich fruit—
The product of the labor of the world—
As he can equal with his own two hands,
His own supply of energy and skill!
As much of Shakespeare,[7] Homer,[8] Socrates,[9]
As much of Wagner,[10] Beethoven,[11] and Bach,[12]
As much of Franklin,[13] Morse,[14] and Edison,[15]
As much of Watt,[16] and Stephenson[17] and Bell,[18]
Of Euclid,[19] Aristotle,[20] Angelo,[21]
Columbus,[22] Raleigh,[23] and George Washington,[24]
Of all the learning of our patient years,
Of all the peace and smoothness we have won,
Of all the heaped up sciences and arts,
And luxuries that man has ever made,—
He is to have what his own toil can match!
Or, passing even this, giving no thought
To this our heritage, our vast bequest,

Condemn him to no more of human help
From living men than he can give to them!
Toil of the soldiers on the western plains,
Toil of the hardened sailors on the sea,
Toil of the sweating ploughman in the field,
The engine-driver, digger in the mine,
And weary weaver in the roaring mill.
Of all the hands and brains and hearts that toil
To fill the world with riches day by day,
Shall he have naught of this but what one man
Can give return for from his own supply?
Brother—There is no payment in the world!
We work and pour our labor at the feet
Of those who are around us and to come.
We live and taking our living at the hands
Of those who are around us and have been.
No one is paid. No person can have more
Than he can hold. And none can do beyond
The power that's in him. To each child that's born
Belong as much of all our human good
As he can take and use to make him strong.
And from each man, debtor to all the world,
Is due the fullest fruit of all his powers,
His whole life's labor, proudly rendered up,
Not as return—can moments pay and age?
But as the simple duty of a man.
Can he do less—receiving everything?

## As Flew the Cross

As flew the fiery cross from hand to hand,
Kindling the scattered people to one flame,
Out-blazing fiercely to a sudden war;
As beacon fires flamed up from hill to hill,
Crying afar to valleys hidden wide
To tell their many dwellers of a fear
That made them one—a danger shadowing all!—
So flies to-day the torch of living fire,
From mouth to mouth, from distant ear to ear;
And all the people of all nations hear;
The printed word, the living word that tells
Of the great glory of the coming day,—
The joy that makes us one forevermore!

## To Labor

Shall you complain who feed the world?
        Who clothe the world?

Who house the world?
Shall you complain who are the world,
    Of what the world may do?
            As from this hour
            You use your power,
    The world must follow you!

The world's life hangs on your right hand!
            Your strong right hand!
            Your skilled right hand!
You hold the whole world in your hand.
    So to it what you do!
            Or dark or light,
            Or wrong or right,
    The world is made by you!

Then rise as you never rose before!
            Nor hoped before!
            Nor dared before!
And show as was never shown before,
    The power that lies in you!
            Stand all as one!
            See justice done!
    Believe, and Dare, and Do!


## Hardly a Pleasure

She had found it dull in her city;
    So had they, in a different mob.
She travelled to look for amusement;
    They travelled to look for a job.

She was loaded with fruit and candy,
    And her section piled with flowers,
With magazine, novels, and papers
    To shorten the weary hours.

Her friends came down in a body
    With farewells merry and sweet,
And left her with laughter and kisses,
    On the broad plush-cushioned seat.

She was bored before she started,
    And the journey was dull and far.
"Travelling's hardly a pleasure!"
    Said the girl in the palace car.[25]

                ‐‐‐‐‐

Then they skulked out in the darkness
    And crawled in under the cars,
To ride on the trucks as best they might,
    To hang by the chains and bars.

None came to see their starting,
    And their friendliest look that day
Was that of a green young brakeman,
    Who looked the other way.

They were hungry before they started,
    With the hunger that turns to pain—
"Travelling's hardly a pleasure,"
    Said the three men under the train.

-----

She complained of the smoke and cinders,
    She complained of the noise and heat,
She complained of the table service,
    She complained of the things to eat.

She said it was so expensive,
    In spite of one's utmost care;
That feeling the porters and waiters
    Cost as much as a third-class fare.

That the seats were dirty and stuffy,
    That the berths were worse by far.
"Travelling's hardly a pleasure!"
    Said the girl in the palace car.

-----

They hung on in desperate silence,
    For a word was a tell-tale shout;
Their foul hats low on their bloodshot eyes,
    To keep the cinders out.

The dirt beat hard on their faces,
    The noise beat hard on their ears,
And a moment's rest to a straining limb
    Meant the worst of human fears.

They clutched and clung in the darkness
    While the stiffness turned to pain.
"Travelling's hardly a pleasure,"
    Said the three men under the train.

-----

She stepped airily out in the morning,
    When the porter had brushed her awhile.
She gave him a silver dollar;
    He gave her an ivory smile.

She complained to her friends that morning
    Of a most distressing dream:
"I thought I heard in the darkness
    A sort of a jolting scream!

"I thought I felt in the darkness
      The great wheels joggle and swing;
Travelling's hardly a pleasure
      When you dream such a horrible thing!"

-----

They crept shuddering out in the morning,
      Red spots with the coal's black stain.
"Travelling's hardly a pleasure!"
      Said the two men under the train.


## Nationalism[26]

The nation is a unit. That which makes
You an American of our to-day,
Requires this nation and its history,
Requires the sum of all our citizens,
Requires the product of our common toil,
Requires the freedom of our common laws,
The common heart of our humanity.
Decrease our population, check our growth,
Deprive us of our wealth, our liberty,
Lower the nation's conscience by a hair,
And you are less than that you were before!
You stand here in the world the man you are
Because your country is America.
Our liberty belongs to each of us;
The nation guarantees it; in return
We serve the nation, serving so ourselves.
Our education is a common right;
The state provides it, equally to all,
Each taking what he can; and in return
We serve the state, so serving best ourselves.
Food, clothing, all necessities of life,—
These are a right as much as Liberty!
The nation feeds its children. In return
We serve the nation, serving still ourselves—
Nay, not ourselves—ourself! We are but parts,
The unit is the state,—America!


## The King is Dead! Long Live the King!

When man, the hunter, winning in the race,
Had conquered much, and, conquering, grown apace,
Till out of victory he found defeat,
And, having eaten all, had naught to eat,—
Then might some Jeremiah[27] sad have said,
Seeing his hopeless case, "The King is dead!"

But man is master most in power to change;
He turned his forest to a cattle range;
There was no foe to strive with—wherefore strive?
No food to kill—he kept his food alive.
Herding his dinner, see him sit and sing
Serene, "The King is dead! Long live the King!"

When man the shepherd, after years did pass,
By nature's increase grew, until the grass
Failed to support the requisite supply
Of cattle who must live lest he should die;
Again a grieved observer might be led
To pitifully say, "The King is dead!"

But man, who turned his prey into a pet,
To outwit hunger, was not baffled yet;
He'd searched for grass so long he'd learned to praise it,
And now that grass was short—why, he could raise it!
His dinner sprouted with the happy spring
Profuse, "The King is dead! Long live the King!"

When man, the farmer, growing very great,
Out of his children built the busy State,
Those greedy children, to his loud alarm,
Pinched all the profits off the old man's farm,
Killing the golden goose,[28] and while he bled,
Cried sage economists, "The King is dead!"

But he, good sooth, was never more alive;
He watched the pools and trusts around him strive,
And when he'd learned the trick—it was not long—
He organized himself—a million strong!
Cornered the food supply! A Farmer's Ring![29]
Hurrah! "The King is dead! Long live the King!"


## "How Many Poor!"

"Whene'er I take my walks abroad, how many poor I see!"
Said pious Watts,[30] and thanked the Lord that not so poor was he.
I see so many poor to-day I think I'll walk no more,
And then the poor in long array come knocking at my door.
The hungry poor! The dirty poor! The poor of evil smell!
Yet even these we could endure if they were only well!
But, O, this sick and crippled crew! The lame, the deaf, the blind!
What can a Christian person do with these upon his mind!
They keep diseases growing still like plants on greenhouse shelves,
And they're so generous they will not keep them to themselves;
They propagate amazing crimes and vices scandalous,
And then at most uncertain times they wreak the same on us!

With charity we would prevent this poverty and woe,
But find the more we've fondly spent, the more the poor do grow!
We've tried by punishment full sore to mend the case they're in;
The more we punish them the more they sin, and sin, and sin!
We make the punishment more kind, we give them wise reform,
And they, with a contented mind, flock to our prisons warm!
Then science comes with solemn air, and shows us social laws,
Explaining how the poor are there from a purely natural cause.
'Tis natural for low and high to struggle and to strive;
'Tis natural for the worse to die and the better to survive.
We swallowed all this soothing stuff, and easily were led
To think if we were stern enough, the poor would soon be dead.
But, O! in vain we squeeze, and grind, and drive them to the wall—
For all our deadly work we find it does not kill them all!
The more we struggle they survive! increase and multiply!
There seem to be more poor alive, in spite of all that die!
Whene'er I take my walks abroad how many poor I see,
And eke at home! How long, O Lord! How long must this thing be!

## The Dead Level

There is a fear among us as we strive,
 As we succeed or fail, or starve or revel,
That there will be no pleasure left alive
When we in peace and joy at last arrive
 At one dead level.

And still the strangest part of this strange fear
 Is that it is not for ourselves we fear it.
We wish to rise and gain; we look ahead
To pleasant years of peace ere we are dead;
 We wish that peace, but wish no other near it!

Say, does it spoil your pleasure in a town
 To have your neighbors' gardens full of roses?
Is your house dearer when its eye looks down
On evil-smelling shanties rough and brown?
 Is your nose safer than your neighbor's nose is?

Are you unhappy at some noble fête
 To see the whole bright throng in radiant dresses?
Is your State safer when each other State
That borders it is full of want and hate?
 Peace must be peace to all before it blesses.

Is knowledge sweeter when it is hemmed in
 By ignorance that does not know its master?
Is goodness easier when plenteous sin
Surrounds it? And can you not win
 Joy for yourself without your friend's disaster?

O foolish children! With more foolish fear,
    Unworthy even of a well-trained devil!
Good things are good for all men,—that is clear;
To doubt it shows your heads are nowhere near
    To that much-dreaded level!

## The Cart Before the Horse

Our business system has its base
On one small thought that's out of place;
    The merest trifle—nothing much, of course.
The truth is there—who says it's not?
Only—the trouble is—you've got
    The cart before the horse!

You say unless a man shall work
Right earnestly, and never shirk
    He may not eat.[31] Now look—the change is small,
And yet the truth is plain to see—
Unless man eats, and frequently,
    He cannot work at all!

And which comes first! Why, that is plain,
The man comes first. And, look again—
    A baby! with an appetite to fit!
You have to feed him years and years,
And train him up with toil and tears,
    Before he works a bit!

So let us change our old ideas,
And learn with these advancing years
    To give the oats before we ask for speed;
Not set the hungry horse to run,
And tell him when the race is done
    That he shall have his feed!

## The Amœboid Cell

Said the Specialized Cell to the Amœboid Cell,[32]
    "Why don't you develop like me?
        Just combine with the others,
        Unite with your brothers,
    And grow to a thing you can see,—
    An organized creature like me!"

Said the Amœboid Cell to the Specialized Cell,
    "But where would my liberty be?
        If I'm one with a class,
        I should lose in the mass

All my Individualities!
And that is a horror to me!"

Said the Specialized Cell to the Amœboid Cell,
"What good does it do you to-day?
You're amorphous and small,
You've got no organs at all,
You can't even get out of the way!
You don't half understand what I say!"

Said the Amœboid Cell to the Specialized Cell,
"But I'm independent and free!
I can float as I please
In these populous seas,
I'm not fastened to anybodee!
I have personal freedom, you see!

"And when I want organs and members and such,
I project them,—an arm or a wing;
I can change as I will,
But you have to keep still—
Just a part of the mass where you cling!
You never can be but one thing!

Said the Specialized Cell to the Amœboid Cell,
"What you say is undoubtedly true,
But I'd rather be part
Of a thing with a heart,
Than the whole of a creature like you!
A memberless morsel like you!

"You say you're immortal and separate and free,
Yet you've died by the billion before;
Just a speck in the slime
At the birthday of time,
And you never can be any more!
As you are, you've no future in store!

"You say you can be many things in yourself,
Yet you're all just alike to the end!
I am part of a whole—
Of a thing with a soul—
And the whole is the unit, my friend!
But that you can scarce comprehend!

"You are only yourself,—just a series of ones;
You can only say 'I'—never 'we';
All of us are combined
In a creature with mind,
And *we* are the creature you see!
And the creature feeds *us*—which is *me*!

"And being combined in a body like that
It can wisely provide us with food;
And we vary and change
In a limitless range;
We are specialized now, for our good!
And we each do our work—as we should!

"What protection have you from the chances of Fate?
What provision have you for the morrow?
You get food when it drops,
And you die when it stops!
You can't give or take, lend or borrow!
You helpless free-agent of sorrow!"

Just then came a frost, and the Amœboid Cell
Died out by the billion again;
But the Specialized Cell
In the body felt well
And rejoiced in his place in the brain!
The dead level of life with a brain!

## The Survival of the Fittest[33]

In northern zones the ranging bear
Protects himself with fat and hair.
Where snow is deep, and ice is stark
And half the year is cold and dark,
He still survives a clime like that
By growing fur, by growing fat.
These traits, O Bear, which thou transmittest,
Prove the survival of the fittest!

To polar regions, waste and wan,
Comes the encroaching race of man;
A puny, feeble little lubber,
He had no fur, he had no blubber.
The scornful bear sat down at ease
To see the stranger starve and freeze;
But, lo! the stranger slew the bear,
And ate his fat, and wore his hair!
These deeds, O Man, which thou committest,
Prove the survival of the fittest!

In modern times the millionaire
Protects himself as did the bear.
Where Poverty and Hunger are,
He counts his bullion by the car.
Where thousands suffer, still he thrives,
And after death his will survives.

The wealth, O Crœsus,[34] thou transmittest
Proves the survival of the fittest!

But, lo! some people, odd and funny,
Some men without a cent of money,
The simple common Human Race,
Chose to improve their dwelling-place.
They had no use for millionaires;
They calmly said the world was theirs;
They were so wise, so strong, so many—
The millionaire? There wasn't any!
These deeds, O Man, which thou committest,
Prove the survival of the fittest!

### Division of Property

Some sailors were starving at sea
On a raft where they happened to be,
  When one of the crew
  Who was hidden from view
Was found to be feasting most free.

Then they cursed him in language profane,
Because there on the pitiless main
  While the others did starve,
  He could ladle and carve,
Eating food which they could not obtain.

"But," said he, "'tis my own little store!
To feed all of you would take more!
  If I shared, 'tis would be found
  That it would not go round;
And you all would starve on as before!

"It would only prolong your distress
To distribute this one little mess!
  The supply is so small
  I had best eat it all,
For me it will comfort and bless!"

This reasoning sounded most fair,
But the men had large appetites there,
  And while he explained
  They ate all that remained,
Forgetting to leave out his share!

### Christian Virtues

Oh, dear!
The Christian virtues will disappear!

Nowhere on land or sea
Will be room for charity!
Nowhere, in field or city,
A person to help or pity!
Better for them, no doubt,
Not to need helping out
Of their old miry ditch.
But, alas for us, the rich!
For we shall lose, you see,
Our boasted charity!—
Lose all the pride and joy
Of giving the poor employ,
And money, and food, and love
(And making stock thereof!).
Our Christian virtues are gone,
With nothing to practice on!

It don't hurt them a bit,
For they can't practice it;
But it's our great joy and pride—
What virtue have we beside?
We believe, as sure as we live,
That it is more blessed to give
Than to want, and waste, and grieve,
And occasionally receive![35]
And here are the people pressing
To rob us of our pet blessing!
No chance to endow or bedizen[36]
A hospital, school, or prison,
And leave our own proud name
To Gratitude and Fame!
No chance to do one good deed,
To give what we do not need,
To leave what we cannot use
To those whom we deign to choose!
When none want broken meat,
How shall our cake be sweet?
When none want flannels and coals,
How shall we save our souls?
Oh, dear! Oh, dear!
The Christian virtues will disappear!

The poor have their virtues rude,—
Meekness and gratitude,
Endurance, and respect
For us, the world's elect;
Economy, self-denial,
Patience in every trial,

Self-sacrifice, self-restraint,—
Virtues enough for a saint!
Virtues enough to bear
All this life's sorrow and care!
Virtues by which to rise
To a front seat in the skies!
How can they turn from this
To common earthly bliss,—
Mere clothes, and food, and drink,
And leisure to read and think,
And art, and beauty, and ease,—
There is no crown for these!
True, if their gratitude
Were not for fire and food,
They might still learn to bless
The Lord for their happiness!
And, instead of respect for wealth,
Might learn from beauty, and health,
And freedom in power and pelf,
Each man to respect himself!
And, instead of scraping and saving,
Might learn from using and having
That man's life should be spent
In a grand development!
But this is petty and small;
These are not virtues at all;
They do not look as they should;
They don't do *us* any good!
Oh, dear! Oh, dear! Oh, dear!
The Christian virtues will disappear!


## What's That?

I met a little person on my land,
    A-fishing in the waters of my stream;
He seemed a man, yet could not understand
    Things that to most men very simple seem.

"Get off!" said I; "this land is mine, my friend!
    Get out!" said I; "this brook belongs to me!
I own the land, and you must make an end
    Of fishing here so free.

"I own this place, the land and water too!
    You have no right to be here, that is flat!
Get off it! That is all I ask of you!—"
    "Own it?" said he; "what's that?"

"What's that?" said I, "why, that is common sense!
     I own the water and the fishing right;
I own the land from here to yonder fence;
     Get off, my friend, or fight!"

He looked at the clear stream so neatly kept;
     He looked at teeming vine and laden tree,
And wealthy fields of grain that stirred and slept;
     "I see!" he cried, "I see!

"You mean you cut the wood and plowed the field,
     From your hard labor all this beauty grew,
To you is due the richness of the yield;
     You have some claim, 'tis true."

"Not so," said I, with manner very cool,
     And tossed my purse into the air and caught it;
"Do I look like a laborer, you fool?
     It's mine because I bought it!"

Again he looked as if I talked in Greek,
     Again he scratched his head and twirled his hat,
Before he mustered wit enough to speak.
     "Bought it?" said he, "what's that?"

And then he said again, "I see! I see!
     You mean that some men toiled with plows and hoes,
And while those worked for you, you toiled with glee
     At other work for those."

"Not so!" said I, getting a little hot,
     Thinking the man a fool as well as funny;
"I'm not a working-man, you idiot;
     I bought it with my money!"

And still that creature stared and dropped his jaw,
     Till I could have destroyed him where he sat.
"Money," said I, "money, and moneyed law!"
     "Money?" said he, "what's that?"


## An Economist

The serene savage sitting in his tree
     Saw empires rise and fall,
And moralized on their uncertainty.
          (He never rose at all!)

He was full fat from god-sent droves of prey;
     He was full calm from satisfied desire;
He was full wise in that he chose to stay
          Free from ambition's fire.

"See," quoth the savage, "how they toil and strive
    To make things better,—vain and idle wish!
Here is good store of what keeps man alive,
    Of fruit, and flesh, and fish.

"Poor discontented wretches, fed on air,
    Seeking to change the normal lot of man,
To lure him from this natural strife and care,
    With vague Utopian plan!

"Here's wealth and joy—why seek for any change?
    Why labor for a more elaborate life?
As if God could not his own world arrange
    Without our fretful strife!

"Those who complain of savagery as low
    Are merely proven lazy, and too weak
To live by skilful hunt and deadly blow;
    It is their needs that speak.

"Complain of warfare! Cry that peace is sweet!
    Complain of hunting! Prate of toil and trade!
It only proves that they cannot compete
    In the free life we've made."

Another empire reeled into its grave;
    The savage sat serenely as before,
As calm and wise, as cunning and as brave—
    Never an atom more.

## Charity

Came two young children to their mother's shelf
    (One was quite little, and the other big),
And each in freedom calmly helped himself.
    (One was a pig.)

The food was free and plenty for them both,
    But one was rather dull and rather small;
So the big smarter brother, nothing loath,
    He took it all.

At which the little fellow raised a yell
    Which tired the other's more æsthetic ears;
He gave him here a crust, and there a shell
    To stop his tears.

He gave with pride, in manner calm and bland,
    Finding the other's hunger a delight;
He gave with piety—his full left hand
    Hid from his right.

He gave and gave—O blessed Charity!
    How sweet and beautiful a thing it is!
How fine to see that big boy giving free
        What is not his!

# Uncollected and Other Poems

## To D[andelion]—— G[reens]——

When first the days are warm and bright,
    When first the blue-birds sing,
When first the wind against the cheek
In subtle odors seems to speak
    Of Memory and Spring:

When tender grass on sunny slopes
    Is thickening day by day,
When baby ferns are half uncurled,
When early sunbeams warm the world,
    And graceful catkins sway;

Then in the meadows cool and wide
    Springeth the flower I love,
And many folk to seek it go,
And cut in carefully below
    And pluck it from above.

A modest plant, and little known
    To those possessed of means:
Yet welcome to the poor man's wife,
The luxury of humble life,
    Is dandelion greens.
        (*New England Journal of Education*, 12 May 1880, 331)


## Young Allan Black

"A nonsense rhyme whereof the sense is plain."[1]

There was a youth who had a horse
    All modified with red.
Said he, "This animal, of course,
    Must have a feather bed."

But while he strode about the mere[2]
    To seek for certain signs,
He came across an engineer
    Who said with piteous whines—

That he was lost and far from home,
    That all his shoes were gone,
That he adored the Church of Rome,[3]
    That he was foreign born.

That he would modestly suggest
    His friend should now advance,
And give to him his hat, and vest,
    His handkerchief and pants.

The youth, whose name was Allan Black,
    Replied with accent good
He hated to expose his back
    To shadows in the wood.

But if his newfound hapless friend
    Would straight with him return,
That he would give him at the end
    As much as he could earn.

And as the fared through wood and wold
    He questioned him full sore;
"And you your elbows every cold?
    And did your father snore?

And can you swing the mighty axe?
    And can you wield a pen?
And would you lay an income tax
    Upon your fellow men?"

The man replied with measured speech
    That he was very chill:—
He laid his finger each or each
    And polkaed on the hill.

And ever as young Allan Black
    Essayed to lead him home,
He cried aloud "I will go back
    Unto the Church of Rome."
        ("In an Old South Church entertainment in Boston Uncle Edward Hale[4]
        actually printed this absolute nonsense."[5] 18 October 1883, Gilman
        Papers, Schlesinger Library, Radcliffe Institute, folder 193)

## Sketches

I.
I can see straight ahead as I lie on the grass.
    Through the bars of a fence green with moss,
A white strip of down where the cloud shadows pass,
    And the sea winds blow coolly across.

A few calves feed and play on the closely cropped turf,
    Or doze in the quivering heat;
There's no noise save the sound of the sand-muffled surf
    And the shrill insect life at our feet.

Far across the brown grass lies a blue, smiling pond,
    In its hollow contentedly curled;
With a bar of bright sand and the ocean beyond,
    A sharp line at the edge of the world.

II.
Deeply the shadow falls, under the mighty walls
    Of ocean-beaten rock;
The water heaves and groans, over its well-worn stones,
    With never ending shock.

Cool is the pleasant breeze, over the pleasant seas,
    Soft is the friendly sky;
Where cloudlets faint and white drift in the azure bright—
    Distant and high.

On a shelving, pebbly beach, beyond the water's reach,
    I sit this summer day;
Watching its ceaseless flow, on the rocky shore below,
    And the tossing of the spray.

And all along the walls, in dainty waterfalls,
    With many a twinkling drop
The little drops run down, across the boulders brown,
    From the meadow land atop.

The sunlight shines and gleams, across the little streams.
    The tide is rising fast;
O may I always keep this chasm cool and deep,
    A picture in my past!
        (Buffalo *Christian Advocate*, 19 June 1884, 2)


## Ode to a Fool

"Let a bear robbed of her whelps meet a man rather than a fool in his folly."
        —*Proverbs* 17:12

Singular insect! Here I watch thee spin
      Upon my pin;
And I know that thou hast not the least idea
      I have thee here.
Strange is thy nature! For thou mayst be slain
      O'er and again,
Dismembered, wasted, torn with tortures hot,
      Yet know it not.
As well pour hate and scorn upon the dead
      As on thy head;
While I discuss thee now I plainly see
      Thee snear at me.

Marvellous creature! What mysterious power
      In idle hour
Arranged the mighty elements whence came
      Thy iron frame!

In every item of thy outward plan
      So like a man—
Yet men are mortal, dying every day,
      While thou dost stay.
The nations rise and die with passing rule;
      But thou, O Fool,
Livedst when drunken Noah a-sleeping lay;[6]
      Livest to-day.

Invulnerable Fool! Thy mind
      Is deaf and blind,
Impervious to sense of sight and smell
      And touch as well.
Thought from without may vainly seek to press
      Thy consciousness;
Man's hard-won knowledge which the ages pile
      But makes thee smile.
Thy vast sagacity and endless din
      Come from within.
Thy voice doth fill the world from year to year;
      Helpless we hear.
Wisdom and wit 'gainst thee have no avail.
      O Fool, all hail!
      (*Kate Field's Washington*, 4 June 1890, 363)

## Ballade of the Young Editor

In the days when I battled to earn
      A supper of crackers and cheese,
I used my poor brain like a churn,
      I labored like any Chinese;
      I toiled like the ants and the bees,
Nor once took my hand from the plough.
      To-day I give afternoon teas—
For I am an editor now!

Then the papers my verses would spurn,
      Magazines, too were *chevaix-de-frise*,[7]
The editors, haughty and stern,
      Sent refusals, as like as green peas;
      They were meant to deter and displease
And dissuade and discourage, I trow!
      No longer I worry and tease—
For I am an editor now!

It shall be an ambition to learn
      How to shun that encroaching disease
Under which solemn editors burn,

Under which young contributors freeze—
    A surfeit of names that one sees
Every day, but no space to allow
    To young writers—*I'll* smile upon these,
For I am an editor now!
      (*Kate Field's Washington*, 18 June 1890, 397)

## Why Nature Laughs

In a very lonely forest,
    Beside a lonely sea,
I found an ancient woman once,
    Beneath an ancient tree.

She was laughing there more wildly
    Than I had ever dreamed.
At first she only sat and shook,
    And then she rolled and screamed.

So I naturally accosted her,
    And asked if I might share
The source of inward merriment
    Which kept her screaming there.

She straightened up and looked at me
    A moment—hardly more—
I seemed to make the lady laugh
    Worse than she did before.

But finally, with gasps for breath,
    And lips that twitched and curled,
Said she: "I'm Grandma Nature,
    And I'm laughing at the world."

"The world!" said I. "The world," said she,
    "Especially *your* half—
I used to rage and grieve for it,
    But now I only laugh.

I used to suffer fearfully
    To see your needless pain,
To see you mortify the flesh
    Because you had a brain.

To see you stultify the brain
    Because you had a soul,
To see you try to save a part
    By injuring the whole.

You stunt the brain with foolishness,
    You stunt the soul with lies,

You stunt the body with disease,
    And then you seek the skies.

You're sickly when you might be well,
    Fools when you might be wise,
And wicked when you might be good,
    Yet you expect the skies.

You hedge yourselves with needless walls,
    You bind with needless chains,
You drive away your natural joys,
    And court unnatural pains.

Why do I laugh?"—she shook again—
    "O dear! O dear! O dear!
Because your hell is such a farce,
    Your heaven is so near."
        (*Pacific Monthly*, 2 [November 1890], 184)


## The Amiable Elephant

In slumber's calm, untroubled joys
    An elephant lay in the sun,
When several small, ungodly boys
Climbed up on him with boisterous noise
    For that was their notion of fun!

No danger in him! He isn't a snake!
    He's a fool, we all can see!
He's too good to hurt us if he were awake—
Too stupid, you mean! The little boys shake
    And hammer their heels in glee!

They twisted his tail and pulled his ears,
    They jumped on him every one—
They pounded his tusks with shouts and jeers
And punched his eyes—the sweet little dears—
    For that was their notion of fun!

I feel a fly! the elephant cried—
    Now see those little boys start!
He rose and he shook from side to side,
And scattered those little boys far and wide,
    In the innocence of his heart.

The elephant found that his feet were red—
    The elephant mild and sweet—
O dear! O dear! the elephant said,
Why, all those nice little boys are dead!
    And he softly wiped his feet.
        (San Francisco *Wasp*, 6 June 1891, 5)

# Mr. Rockefeller's Prayer

The wealthy Mr. Rockefeller is reported to have said that his income was so very much in excess of his means of spending it that he had to kneel down every day and ask for Divine guidance to get rid of it.[8]

By his bedside, bowed in prayer,
Kneeleth the multi-millionaire—
Rockefeller, the millionaire.

He that believeth! He that prays!
Asking the Lord to show him ways
To spend his gold—to Him the praise!

For it pileth up and it lieth loose—
Surplus gold beyond his use
From the virgin's lamp[9] and the widow's cruse.[10]

"Teach me, Lord, how I may spend
This gold of mine that has no end—
Shall I buy? Buy what? Shall I give? Or lend?"

Answers the Lord of spirit pure
Out of the word that shall endure—
"Sell all thou hast and give the poor!"[11]

But this man that hath lain strong hand
On the people's oil, on the people's land,
Wealth-blinded—can he understand?

We give him wealth, whoever we be,
We pay his price in this land of the free,
And he selleth for less across the sea![12]

They pay less and we pay more,
Helpless all on either shore,
And still upswelleth his mighty store.

It swelleth vast and it weigheth sore,
It rolleth and doubleth o'er and o'er,
And so he prayeth—listen once more!

"Teach me, Lord, what I must do
To spend my gold and pleasure you—
To hold the earth and heaven too!"

Answers the Lord of pain so free—
The Lord of love and poverty—
"Take up thy cross and follow me!"[13]

While his unspent gold doth vex his head,
While a million children cry for bread,
How shall he hear what the Lord hath said?

In the name of the hungry left unfed,
Or the sick and in prison unvisited,
Listen to what the Lord hath said!

His Heaven is not reached by sin,
The meek and the poor its crown may win,
But the rich shall hardly enter in!

Pray, thou rich man! Pray again!
To the Lord of poverty and pain;
Pray and do—his Word is plain!
                (San Francisco *Wasp*, 21 November 1891, 2)


## "The Poor Ye Have Always With You"[14]

The poor ye have always with you—therefore why
        See to improve a lot ordained of God—
        Dare to rebel beneath his chastening rod—
Question the law on high?

The poor ye have always with you—plain to see
        Is this thing so far—stated by our Lord,
        Proved the fact and also by his Word—
So it must surely be.

Yet wait—"have always" is the present tense
        He said they had them always, and they had,
        Must we therefore believe a thing so bad
Shall always crush us with its weight immense?

"You always have the headache!" I complain—
        'Tis not prediction that you always will,
        Nor yet a lasting curse to say, worse still,
That you must always bear that pain.

The poor we had had with us in full store
        From senseless age to age. Let man to-day
        Rise up and put this human shame away—
Let us have poor no more!
                (Boston *New Nation*, 4 June 1892, 356)


## To Mothers

In the name of your ages of anguish!
In the name of the curse and the stain!
By the strength of your sorrow I call you!
        By the power of your pain!

We are Mothers. Through us in our bondage,
Through us with the brand in the face—

Be we fettered with gold or with iron—
    Through us comes the race!

With the weight of all sin on our shoulders,
Midst the serpents of shame ever curled,
We have sat, unresisting, defenseless,
    Making the men of the world.

We were ignorant long, and our children
Were besotted and brutish and blind,
King-driven, priest-ridden—who were they?
    Our children—mankind!

We were kept for our beauty, our softness,
Our sex;—what reward do ye find?
We transmit, must transmit, being mothers,
    What we are to mankind!

As the mother, so follow the children!
No nation, wise, noble, and brave,
Ever sprang—though the father had freedom—
    From the mother—a slave!

Look now at the world as ye find it!
Blench not! Truth is kinder than lies!
Look now at the world—see it suffer!
    Listen now to its cries!

See the people who suffer—all people!
All humanity wasting its powers
In a hand to hand struggle, death-dealing—
    All children of ours!

The blind millionaire—the blind harlot—
The blind preacher leading the blind—[15]
Only think of their pain, how it hurts them!
    Our little blind babies—mankind!

Shall we bear it, we mothers who love them?
Can we bear it, we mothers who feel
Every pang of our babes, and forgive them
    Every sin when they kneel?

Little stumbling world! You have fallen!
You are crying in darkness and fear!
Wait, darling—your mother is coming!
    Hush, darling—your mother is here!

We are here like an army with banners,
The great flag of our freedom unfurled!
With us rests the fate of the nations.
    For we make the world!

Dare ye sleep while your children are calling?
Dare ye wait while they clamor unfed?
Dare ye pray in the proud pillared churches
    While they suffer for bread?

If the father hath sinned, he shall answer;
If he check thee, laugh back at his powers.
Shall a mother be kept from her children?
    These people are ours!

They are ours! He is ours, for we made him!
In our arms he has nestled and smiled!
Shall we, the world-mothers, be hindered
    By the freaks of a child?

Rise now, in the power of The Woman!
Rise now, in the hour of our need!
The world cries in hunger and darkness!
    We shall light! We shall feed!

In the name of our ages of anguish;
In the name of the curse and the stain;
By the strength of our sorrow we conquer!—
    In the power of our pain!
        (*In This Our World*, I, 37–39)

## Ballade of ye Gentil Mayde

Shee was a mayde, a gentil mayde,
    Her hearte was softe and kynde,
And yet shee liked her forse's tayle
    Cut off behynde, behynde—
    Cut off full shorte behynde.

With blynders, checks, and martyngales
    That hapless beaste was tyde,
Or else her sadylle galled his backe
    Whenever shee did ryde.
    O why not sit astride?

Shee had a dogge, a lyttel dogge,
    Shee wore him on a chayne,
Shee made him fatte, she made him sickke,
    And so he dyed in payne—
    Alas, he dyed in payne!

Shee had a flower, a lovely flower,
    Which languished in a potte,
Shee tho't it was its nature to—
    But then you know it's notte!
    Of course we know it's notte!

She had a byrde, a yellow byrde,
    Life-prisoned in a cayge!
'Tis naught, sayth shee, because you see
    He was born in that same cayge—
    Or caught at a tender ayge.

As if, ofsooth, when men were slaves,
    It added to their glee
To have theyre sires, and eke themselves,
    Born into slaveree!
    Born fast in slaveree!

But O this mayde! This gentil mayde!
    Shee wore upon her hedde
A hatte the ornaments of which
    Were bodies of the dedde!
    Just fragments of the dedde!

The feathers of dedde byrdes shee wore.
    Tayles of the slaughtered beaste.
Theyre lyttel heddes her buttons were
    Shee wore a score at leaste!
    A score of deaths at leaste!

O gentil mayde! O lovely mayde!
    With mylde and tender eye!
Why is is for youre pleasuring
    These lyttel ones must dye?
    These helpless ones must dye?
      (*In This Our World*, I, 44–45)


## Vain Fears

O fools and blind! Are ye so wed to pain
That pleasure seems a weariness and waste!
Is vice so dear that you must fling disdain
    On virtue, angel-faced!

Doth foul disease make glad life fly so fast
    That death appears a dull and tedious guest?
Are care and labor grown so sweet at last
    Ye dare scorn ease and rest?

If man and maid and child are free and strong
And grew in power and knowledge year by year,
Free from the fear of want, the fear of wrong,
    Who loses? Why this fear?

They would not suffer who had ne'er before
Known aught but care and hunger, toil and pain;

Who loses them, but ye who now have more
    Then all their lifetime's gain?

What do ye lose? Only the power to shine
Light against darkness, triumph o'er defeat,
The dismal "yours" beside the glorious "mine!"—
    That contrast passing sweet.

Yet 'neath this folly is a saving grace,
An underlying truth, deep as the sea—
We know that Pain is Pleasure's other face—
    A twofold mystery.

We know there is no light save shade be there,
No wisdom without folly hid within,
No strength without some weakness to compare,
    No virtues without sin.

But the soul grows, the pains and pleasures change,
Age after age we need, and Nature gives;
Mankind still rises in his ceaseless range;
    The human creature lives!

Did they dread loss who changed the awful cold
For fire, with train of torture and disease?
Or nakedness for dress, with sin less bold?
    There was no loss in these!

'Twas gain to change the freedom of the hills
For homes; to live by fraud instead of force;
'Twas gain to change brute passions, wed at will,
    For marriage—and divorce!

Fear not, O fools! The pathway must be trod!
Who fights with fate will ever fight in vain;
Take your new pleasures at the hand of God—
    He will provide new pain!
        (*In This Our World*, I, 80–81)


## A Hope

Are you tired, patient miner?[16]
        Digging slowly in the dark
With your tiny pick and shovel
        At the wall of granite stark—

The awful wall of ignorance
        The iron wall of sin,
The mountain weight that crowds you down
        And holds you darkly in?

Does your gain seem less than nothing—
    All in vain the work you do—
While you can't get out as you got in,
    And yet cannot get through?

Then listen to a word of hope—
    'Tis not about the sky—
'Tis not to bid you bear all this
    For a ghostly by and by—

'Tis to tell you there is help at hand,
    While there alone you bow;
That the daylight clear is coming near—
    Yes, it is coming now!

Brave digger in your narrow hole
    In that great wall of stone—
Be of good cheer—the end is near—
    You have not worked alone!

Listen! Before—behind you—
    Above—below—around—
A million miners rend the rock
    With rolling waves of sound!

A million hands are tearing fast—
    The rock is growing thin—
And soon the human heart shall range
    Beyond the walls of sin!
        (*In This Our World*, I, 105–6)


## News

Crieth the empty public, greedily,
    "I want the news!
And they who write and publish, needily,
Come running to his cry, and fill him speedily
    With what they choose.

With all that they can steal or beg or borrow
    Of crimes and shames,
Serving prodigious tales of sin and sorrow
That happened yesterday and will to-morrow,
    With different names.

The newest murder heads the blackened pages
    With spreading stains.
News? Is it news to know the lion rages?
Your newest murder smells of oldest ages,
    As old as Cain's.

News of a man's defencelessness—temptation—
    (Which all believe)—
News of a woman's sudden education
In good and evil's fine discrimination—
    As old as Eve!

We want real news—not tales of dying, wooing,
    And such old lore—
We want to hear of big events now brewing,
We want to know the things the world is doing.
    Not done before.

The world would be pleased with less of daring,
    If it could choose;
With less of private life hung out for airing—
Mere nursery tales in which we all are sharing—
    And more real news.

News! World-old tales of man's first freaks and poses,
    Primal mistakes.
They cannot see the news before their noses—
Only these fresh, the crowded sheet discloses—
    Some brand-new fakes!
        (*Impress*, 20 October 1894, 5)


## The Duty Farthest

Finding myself unfit to serve my own,
I left them, sadly, and went forth alone
    Unto the world where all things wait to do—
    The harvest ripe—the laborers but few.
I studied long to find the wisest way,
Proved every step, worked on day after day
    In those great common tasks that need us all
    But where one's own part is so brief and small
That no one counts the labor one has spent
Yet I could see good grow and was content.
    Ah me! I sighed, for home served lovingly.
    And lo! the whole round world was home to me.
        (*Impress*, 17 November 1894, 5)


## Tassels

Don't you remember the tassels that hung
    By grandma's window pane
When the curtains, as old as you were young,
Worked with a cord by the casing strung,
    And fuzzy tassels twain.

The big one holding a chunk of lead,
  The light one light and free,
Hard little branches for hips and head
A silk-wound body stiff and dead,
  And the cords swung merrily.

We used to hold it around the waist
  And make it dance with glee,
Whichever way the thing was placed
A human semblance might be traced
  In the cord-fringed mystery.

Dear tassels! I can see them now,
  Joy of the childish mind;
I like to watch them dance and bow
And walk, to show each other how,
  Bending before—behind.

And still we see them, year by year,
  By them our streets are graced,
The rounded shoulders swelling clear;
The rounded hips we hold so dear,
  The silk-bound wooden waist.

And swinging skirts that as they go,
  Rock free from side to side,
And swingeth swiftly to and fro
Suggesting tassel's wavy flow;
  But not a soul inside.
      (*Impress*, 1 December 1894, 4)


## A New Creation

What is that, mother? A head, my child,
  The house of a human brain;
A windowed musical palace of thought
By whose clear light the world was brought
  To all its growth and gain.

What is that, mother? 'Tis hair, my child,
  Long beautiful human hair,
Whose parallel grace of curve and flow
Is cut and twisted and tortured so
  You doubt it ever was there.

What is that, mother? A hat, my child,
  To cover a human head;
Shelter and grace for the house of the brain—
With colors or discord and lines of pain
  And ornaments from the dead.

What is that, mother? I do not know,
    The milliner finds it fair;
Over head and hair and hat they grow,
Tail, tooth and claw, wing, plume, and bow,
Silk, velvet, lace, and jewel's glow,
Fur flowers, ribbon, beads a-row,
Aigrette, rosette, and bright bandau—
    A new creation there.

Rejoice in your big Christmas tree,
    My happy little lad,
And wonder not that most of us
    Are hungry, sour, and sad.

What's that you say, my little son?
    Christ came to teach us love—
Love all the time, for every one,
    And the great joy thereof?

I grant you that it reads that way,
    But who are you to stand
Against the wisdom of the day
    In every Christian land?

Here are the facts, my little son—
    And facts are stubborn things;
Judge if the state of man to-day
    Is what the angel sings.
        (*Impress*, 15 December 1894, 5)


## Christmas Time

'Tis Christmas time, my little son,
    The birthday of the Lord,
Who said he came to bring on earth
    Not peace, dear, but a sword.

"Peace and good will," the angels sing
    On the birthday of the Lord;
But Christ declared he came to bring
    Not peace, dear, but a sword.

He said he came to set the son
    At variance with his sire,
And that a man's foes should be found
    Around his household fire.

So it is right that we should see,
    On the birthday of the Lord,
In a million hearts a million hates,
    In a million hands a sword.

No wonder that our homes are rent,
    That brother hateth brother,
No wonder that our lives are spent
    In ruining each other.

No wonder that the most of men
    Still hunt and fight for good—
The wonder is that any one
    Is ever half so good.

But this is Christmas time, my son,
    Go get your broken toys,
And give to the ungrateful hands
    Of poorer girls and boys.
        (*Impress*, 22 December 1894, 5)


## Ideas. (After Emerson)[17]

We do not makes ideas: they flow
From wondrous unknown gulfs behind,
Down into the receptive mind.
We seize them as they go
And seek to clothe the naked thought,
Each with what skill his trade hath taught,
In picture, music, pile of stone,
Statue, or book, or speech alone,
That we may keep and share it so.

Who faileth to arrest—
The formless flying guest
Is left forlorn;
Later, he sees the face
That once his dreams did grace,
Drawn by another's hand
In deathless beauty stand,
And thinks—"To *me* this child was born!"[18]
        (*In This Our World*, II, 107)


## The Teacher

Who leads the world in its long upward way?
    Who rules the world with scepter still unknown?
    Who, above all, should we devoutly own
As leader, and our gladdest tribute pay?

The sword no longer holds its iron sway,
    The monarch in tradition sits alone;
    The growth of man in a child's eyes is shown,
And whoso leads the child, leads us to-day.

Administrator of man's highest power,
    His noblest art, his first prerogative,
    And the most blessed joy in life—to give!
Give the mind truth, like water to a flower;
So gives the teacher. Praise and tribute bring—
The teacher is the leader and the king!
        (*In This Our World*, II, 108)


## The San Francisco Hen

The San Francisco house-mama
    A happy dame is she,
When feeding to her gathered young
    The fragrant fricassee,
The amber broth for invalids
    Rich broilers for the men,
        With boiled, and roast,
        And hash on toast,
    Of the San Francisco hen.

But walk the wholesale market streets
    Ye housewives kind and wise,
And on the poultry set for sale
    Fix your discerning eyes;
In crowded cages huddled down
    Unwatered and unfed
        In fear and pain,
        In sun and rain,
    They scream till they are dead.

They live in filth and agony,
    They die in shrieking fear—
Come down, ye guardians of the home,
    And see and smell and hear!
Let not your hearts be troubled
    By the tortures you behold,
        But judge if meat
        Is good to eat
    Defiled before it's sold.

The meekest housewife may assume
    An interest in the health
Of those about her board who earn—
    Who are the country's wealth;
And meat like this means vile disease
    Among the sons of men—
        Not to dilate

On the ghastly fate
Of the San Francisco hen.
(*Impress*, 26 January 1895, 5)


## In Re "Andromaniacs"[19]

Parkhurst says that woman is superior,
Man, her son, confessedly inferior;
That Scripture prove her excellence interior—
    "God's favorite sex" is she;
Pray forgive the scientific quierier
    Who asks how that can be.

He says 'tis not in the body or the mind of her,
But an element constituent in all that you can find of her,
Not to see it is obdurate and blind of her;
    Stupid as can be;
She is queen because of it—truly, more than kind of her!
    Queen of man is she.

She is best, because of femininity.
Man, poor wretch, has only masculinity.
Here stands forth this servant of the Trinity
    To show which God prefers—
The crowns and palms and prizes of infinity
    Undoubtedly are hers.

Still poor man may rule the world and fight in it,
Teach and preach and hold his little light in it,
Toil and plan that living may be bright in it,
    All for the sake of love;
She has only to keep from any right in it,
    To hold her place above.
(*Impress*, 2 February 1895, 4)


## My Cyclamen

A little dull brown bulb from somewhere,
    And out of its heart,
For days and months together,
With never a thought for time or weather,
    The white buds start.

Great green lovely leaves surround it,
    Shaped like a heart,
Large green leaves with purple under,
And when they fall—the living wonder!—
    Fair new ones start.

No matter now for air or sunlight,
    Alone it lives.
Once 'twas fed with a flower's full blessing,
And from that memory caressing
    It gives and gives!

Crowding up in their generous beauty
    The white buds start;
Once made rich with the joy of living—
Now it has more in giving and giving
    Out of its heart.
        (*Impress*, 9 February 1895, 4)


## Work and Wages

John Burns[20] receives in weekly pay
    Five pounds as wages, clear;
But a London banker, wise and great,
Says John is worth to the English state
    Three million pounds a year.

He gives three million pounds in work,
    Gets fifty-two times five;
It does not seem exactly straight
That he who serves so well the state
    Should just be kept alive.

John Rockefeller corners oil,[21]
    To make thereby a living;
And, by an odd coincidence,
He makes—an income most immense—
    Just what John Burns is giving.

He gives—the skill to corner oil!
    Gets fifteen million yearly;
(Dollars for pounds the sum's the same,)
But how in all creation's name,
    Does it come to match so queerly?

The rich man makes his yearly claim,
    John Burns' labor meets it;
But why should one man feed the earth,
Enriching it by all he's worth,
    If Rockefeller eats it?

And why should Rockefeller have,
    For handing round the oil,
For his own self in private wealth
Fruit of the teeming strength and health
    Of such unstinted toil?

John Burns is rich and feeds the world,
    The world will soon forget him;
John Rockefeller, poor and lean,
Licks all our fullest platters clean—
    It's funny that we let him!
        (*Impress*, 9 February 1895, 4)


## Ruined

I am ruined! sobbed the seed,
    As it fell, by free winds shaken;
For the earth was dark indeed,
    All the light and heat were taken,
All the birds' songs and leaves' laughter—
Only silence followed after—
    Cold and darkness were its meed.

I am ruined! cried the rock
    As it fell in fragments scattered,
For its strength went with the shock.
    All its use on earth was shattered;
All its grandeur and stern beauty,
All its forest-bearing duty—
    Lost in many a shapeless block.

I am ruined! wept the woman
    As she fell by Love's beguiling,
For her fate was fierce, inhuman;
    All hope vanished, sadly smiling,
All the chance of reinstatement,
Only shame without abatement,
    Endless shame for fallen woman.

After seedtime came the sun,
    And warm rains of spring caressing,
Till the seed that was but one
    Grew into a tree of blessing,
Feeding, shading, emerald-suited
Rosy-blossomed, golden-fruited—
    Joy of all it shone upon.

The torn rock lay far and wide,
    Hammered sore and carved and hollowed
Till a temple rose beside,
    And fair palaces that followed.
Power and beauty crowned the portals,
Shelter to a race of mortals—
    Long the rock was glorified.

And the woman? She rose brave,
　　　Learned new wisdom from old sorrow,
Wide that costly wisdom gave
　　　For all helpless ones to borrow—
Purer for the fiery trial,
Stronger for the long denial,
　　　Soul re-made to help and save.
　　　　　(*In This Our World*, III, 124–25)


## Morning

Think not of the morning as coming and going,
　　　　Growing out of the dark,
　　　　Growing into the day—
While your place in the circle is lit by the glowing
　　　Which cometh and passeth away.

But see the green circle still turning and turning,
　　　　While the sun never faileth
　　　　Wherever earth flies;
The light poureth steady—the earth turneth ready—
　　　And the glory of morning on earth never dies.

Like the crest of a wave combing white o'er green hollows,
　　　　Sweeps the crest of the morning
　　　　Around the green world,
And dawn-music rolls up in the path that it follows
　　　With bright flowers unfolded and light wings unfurled.
　　　　　(*In This Our World*, III, 147)


## Women to Men. Relatives and Otherwise

Dear father, from my cradle I acknowledge
All your wise kindness, tender care, and love,
Through days of kindergarten, school, and college.
Now there is one gift lacking—one above
All other gifts of God, this highest trust is,
The one great gift, beyond all power and pelf—
Give me my freedom, father; give me justice,
That I may guard my children and myself.

My brother, you and I were reared together;
We played together, even-handed quite;
We went to school in every kind of weather,
Studied and ranked together as was right.
We work together now and earn our living,
You know how equal is the work we do;

Come, brother, with the love you're always giving,
Give justice! It's for me as well as you.

And you, my lover, kneeling here before me
With tender eyes that burn, warm lips that plead,
Protesting that you worship, aye, adore me;
Begging my love as life's supremest meed,
Vowing to make me happy. Ah, how dare you!
Freedom and happiness have both one key!
Lover and husband, by the love I bear you,
Give justice! I can love you better, free!

Son, my own son! Man-child that once was lying
All rosy, tender, helpless on my breast,
Your strength, all dimples, your stern voice but crying,
Looking to me for comfort, food and rest,
Asking your life of me, and not another—
And asking not in vain till life be done—
Oh, my boy-baby! Is it I, your mother,
Who comes to ask of justice from her son?

Now to the voter—tax-payer (or shirker)
Please lay your private feelings on the shelf;
O Man-at-large! Friend! Comrade! Fellow-worker;
I am a human being like yourself.
I'm not your wife and mother. Can't be, whether
I would or not: each to his own apart;
But in the world we're people altogether—
Suffrage is not a question of the heart.

Son—Father—Brother—Lover unsupplanted—
We'll talk at home. This thing concerns the nation;
A point of justice which is to be granted
By men to women who are no relation.
Perceive this fact, as salient as a steeple,
Please try to argue from it if you can;
Women have standing-room on earth as people
Outside of their relation to some man.

As wife and sweetheart, daughter, sister, mother,
Each woman privately her views explains;
As people of America—no other—
We claim the right our government maintains.
You who deny it stand in history's pages
Withholding justice! Pitiless and plain
Your record stands down all the brightening ages—
You fought with progress, but you fought in vain.
                    (*Woman's Journal*, 1 February 1896, 33)

## For the New Year

For the New Year,
The year which is not yet come;
The year we wait and pray,
Each hoarse and strenuous day,
Each short night blind and dumb,
May bring more near.

The year of our Lord!
When he shall come again;
Come in his love and ruth,
Come in spirit and truth,
Making an end of pain,
Breaking the spear and sword!

For the year of Man!
Of man awake and free;
Man, who shall stand at last
Clear of the blinding past,
And breathe and see—
See that he is a Man!

For the year of Woman, too!
Woman, a slave no more;
Woman, no longer fed
On dependence bitter bread;
No longer suffering sore—
Woman, with love born new!

For the year of the Child!
Reared in Freedom and Light;
Ah! if you could but dream
Of what the world would seem
When childhood has its right!
We do not know the Child!

Come! for our passionate tears!
Come! while we work and pray;
And lo! as we strive, the light
Kindles across the night—
The dawn of the coming day!
The Day of the Year of Years!
   (*American Fabian*, 3 [January 1897], 8)


## Our System

When our economic system wore the cowl,
With the golden keys of heaven in its hand,
When it governed all the people from the overarching sky,
And made us all believe what we could not understand—

Why we reverenced the cowl and the keys upon our knees—
And naturally the system kept the churchmen at their ease—
While the people could but labor, pray, and die.

When our economic system wore the crown,
And held the golden scepter in its hand,
When it governed all the people from the guarded throne so high,
And made us all obey what we could not understand—
Why we reverenced the crown and the scepter on our knees,
And naturally the system kept the nobles at their ease—
While the people could but labor, fight, and die.

Now our economic system wears a hat—
And has nothing but its money in its hand.
Now it governs all the people from the fields that 'round us lie,
Well justified by learned books we cannot understand—
Still we reverence the power and the money on our knees,
And naturally the system keeps the rich men at their ease—
While the people can but labor, vote, and die.

But our economic system is our own!
We have made it with the toil of head and hand!
We have made and we can change it! We do not need to give
All our substance to this brother here who will not understand!
We must all work on together, on our feet and not our knees!
And our remodelled system will keep all the world with ease—
While the people all can labor, vote, and live!
          (*American Fabian*, 3 [July 1897], 8)


## To American Men

Men! Men! Front of the foremost race!
      In this day's fight
      For truth and right
Show you deserve your place!

Lead! Lead! You have led the world so long
      O, shall it be said
      When we are dead
That we could not meet this wrong.

Shame! Shame! Never shall this be told,
      That American men
      Were slaves again
To the power of purse and gold!

Rise! Rise! As you rose against the king!
      As once the crown
      You trampled down,
Throw down the trust and ring!

Learn! Learn! The truth is plain to see!
    While the few can take
    What the many make
The country is not free!

Vote! Vote! The world will understand!
    You need not kill
    To work your will—
The ballot is in your hand!

Now! Now! Now and ever again!
    You have the power—
    You know the hour—
O, strong American men!
        (Chicago *Social Democrat*, 25 November 1897, 2)


## Our Wealth

How poor I am! Cries one whose hold
    Is scant of gold,
And whose sole share of earth's supply
    That gold must buy.

And even he, the millionaire,
    Has naught to spare,
But must spend much and struggle brave
    The rest to save;

To fence and wall and guard his pile,
    Fearing the while
Lest, in the safest place where he can set it,
    Some one will get it!

How rich we are! We all shall cry
    When by and by
The wide world's wealth lies in the sun
    For every one!

Finding that what we most would own
    No man alone
Can use; all, using, leave the store
    Enriched the more!

The earth our garden—sea to sea
    Pleasure-ground free!
All man's glad fruit of varied powers
    Openly ours!

Each one exulting in the thought
    Of joy unbought;

Born to the throne, each kingdom found
   Horizon-bound!

Inclusive wealth! Where each is guest
   To all the rest!
All co-possessors of the common weal,
   Which none can steal!

Courteous we offer the uncounted store—
   There's plenty more!
Gladly we labor for an easy while
   To swell the pile;

Rich, safe, forever free from poor,
   Our peace secure,
And each man as his fortune's worth—
   Owning the earth!
         (*American Fabian*, 4 [March 1898], 3)


## Our Tomorrow

Back of our wide world-curving waste of land
      Back of the questioning unanswered sea;
The home of Memory, whose heavy hand
      Still drags the past with each slow step to be;
Tradition, with its load of pride and shame,
Holding each timid century the same;
Moving in dreams, forgotten, far away,
Like yesterday—the land of yesterday!

On our first coast where still the ships pour in
      Blood of all nations, here in one to flow;
In swift transitions where each soul may win
      Only a moment's chance to strike a blow;
The past still clinging to their country's hem,
The future stirring strangely under them:
Nor back they look, nor forward, nor away—
Here is today   the land of sharp today.

But we? Our land lies large. The sunlight stays
      Behind us nothing and before us all.
Here without haste we enter the wide ways
      Where the clear voices of the future call.
No dead hand holds us; we are not shut in
By brooding memories of what has been.
We are not hurried; here the years roll free;
Nature has peace, and so, at last, have we.

Rich with the past in all its storied length;
Proud in the present, glorying in its strength;

Most blessed of all times, all men, all lands—
We hold the world's tomorrow in our hands.
(*Land of Sunshine*, 8 [May 1898], 251)

## America

Rich with the past in all its storied length;
Proud in the present, glorying in its strength;
Most blessed of all times, all men, all lands—
We hold the world's to-morrow in our hands!
(*Youth's Companion*, 25 August 1898, 34)

## The Rats of Ruskin

O Ruskin colony's fair to see,[22]
And full of promise and pride.
But there is a worm at the heart of the rose,
A skeleton hid, that we now disclose,
A dangerous, villainous foe have we—
A traitorous foe inside.

When Ruskin colony sleeps at last,
When the echoing boards are still
When still are the dishes, the chairs, the feet,
And even the steam-pipes cease to heat,
What is this galloping wild and fast?
The RATS are out with a will!

The rats that riot in Ruskin halls
And fatten like pigs in pen;
The rats that feed on the Ruskin stores,
The rats that race on the Ruskin floors,
The rats that gnaw through the Ruskin walls
And defy the Ruskin men!

Women, they say, are afraid of mice—
Clutching their petticoats' hem—
But what shall we say in a case so plain?
Eight MEN cooks in Ruskin reign;
Their arms are strong and their food is nice,
BUT THE RATS RULE OVER THEM!

Are there no colony dogs in sight?
Or a breed of big, colony cats?
Is there never a trap more ingenious than they?
Is there never a poison will clear them away?
Is there never a hero to rise in his might
And save our dear Ruskin from RATS!
(Ruskin, Tenn., *Coming Nation*, 11 February 1899, 4)

## Eternal Me

What an exceeding rest 'twill be
When I can leave off being Me!
To think of it!—at last be rid
Of all the things I ever did!

Done with the varying distress
Of retroactive consciousness!
Set free to feel the joy unknown
Of Life and Love beyond my own!
Why should I long to have John Smith
Eternally to struggle with?
I'm John—but somehow cherubim
Seems quite incongruous with him.

It would not seem so queer to dwell
Eternally John Smith in Hell.
To be one man forever seems
Most fit in purgatorial dreams.

But Heaven! Rest and Power and Peace
Must surely mean the soul's release
From this small labeled entity—
This passing limitation—Me!
(*Cosmopolitan*, 27 [September 1899], 477)


## Too Wise

For those who hold a righteous rage,
    And blame the sinner sore:
It does not do to grow too wise,
    And see what went before—
One cannot comfortably hate
    The sinner any more.

For those who love to teach the world,
    And show mankind the way,
Who learn to preach acceptably,
    And find their preachments pay:
It does not do to grow too wise—
    There's so much less to say!
(*Philistine*, 12 [May 1901], 6)


## Self-Conceit

To think one's own all-adequate
Is ignorance indeed.
(*Youth's Companion*, 11 December 1902, 50)

## Two Callings

I

I hear a deep voice through uneasy dreaming,
    A deep, soft, tender, soul-beguiling voice;
A lulling voice that bids the dreams remain,
That calms my restlessness and dulls my pain,
That thrills and fills and holds me till in seeming
    There is no other sound on earth—no choice.

"Home!" says the deep voice, "Home!" and softly singing
    Brings me a sense of safety unsurpassed;
So old! so old! The piles above the wave—
The shelter of the stone-blocked, shadowy cave—
Security of sun-kissed treetops swinging—
    Safety and Home at last!

"Home" says the sweet voice, and warm Comfort rises,
    Holding my soul with velvet-fingered hands;
Comfort of leafy lair and lapping fur,
Soft couches, cushions, curtains, and the stir
Of easy pleasures that the body prizes,
    Of soft, swift feet to serve the least commands.

I shrink—half rise—and then it murmurs "Duty!"
    Again the past rolls out—a scroll unfurled;
Allegiance and long labor due my lord—
Allegiance in an idleness abhorred—
I am the squaw—the slave—the harem beauty—
    I serve and serve, the handmaid of the world.

My soul rebels—but hark! a new note thrilling,
    Deep, deep, past finding—I protest no more;
The voice says "Love!" and all those ages dim
Stand glorified and justified in him;
I bow—I kneel—the woman soul is willing—
    "Love is the law. Be still! Obey! Adore!"

And then—an, then! The deep voice murmurs "Mother!"
    And all life answers from the primal sea;
A mingling of all lullabies; a peace
That asks no understanding; the release
Of nature's holiest power—who seeks another?
    Home? Home is Mother—Mother, Home—to me.

"Home!" says the deep voice; "Home and Easy Pleasure!
    Safety and Comfort, Laws of Life well kept!
Love!" and my heart rose thrilling at the word;
"Mother!" it nestled down and never stirred;
"Duty and Peace and Love beyond all measure!
    Home! Safety! Comfort! Mother!"—and I slept.

II
A bugle call! A clear, keen, ringing cry,
     Relentless—eloquent—that found the ear
Through fold on fold of slumber, sweet, profound—
A widening wave of universal sound,
Piercing the heart—filling the utmost sky—
     I wake—I must wake! Hear—for I must hear!

"The World! The World is crying! Hear its needs!
     Home is a part of life—I am the whole!
Home is the cradle—shall a whole life stay
Cradled in comfort through the working day?
I too am Home—the Home of all high deeds—
     The only Home to hold the human soul!

"Courage!—the front of conscious life!" it cried;
     "Courage that dares to die and dares to live!
Why should you prate of safety? Is life meant
In ignominious safety to be spent?
Is Home best valued as a place to hide?
     Come out, and give what you are here to give!

"Strength and Endurance! of high action born!"
     And all that dream of Comfort shrank away,
Turning its fond, beguiling face aside:
So Selfishness and Luxury and Pride
Stood forth revealed, till I grew fierce with scorn,
     And burned to meet the dangers of the day.

"Duty? Aye, Duty! Duty! Mark the word!"
     I turned to my old standard. It was rent
From hem to hem, and through the gaping place
I saw my undone duties to the race
Of man—neglected—spurned—how had I heard
     That word and never dreamed of what it meant!

"Duty! Unlimited—eternal—new!"
     And I? My idol on a petty shrine
Fell as I turned, and Cowardice and Sloth
Fell too, unmasked, false Duty covering both—
While the true Duty, all-embracing, high,
     Showed the clear line of noble deeds to do.

And then the great voice rang out to the sun,
     And all my terror left me, all my shame,
While every dream of joy from earliest youth
Came back and lived!—that joy unhoped was truth,
All joy, all hope, all truth, all peace grew one,
     Life opened clear, and Love? Love was its name!

So when the great word "Mother!" rang once more,
    I saw at least its meaning and its place;
Not the blind passion of the brooding past,
But Mother—the World's Mother—come at last,
To love as she had never loved before—
    To feed and guard and teach the human race.

The world was full of music clear and high!
    The world was full of light! The world was free!
And I? Awake at last, in joy untold,
Saw Love and Duty broad as life unrolled—
Wide as the earth—unbounded as the sky—
    Home was the World—the World was Home to me!
        (from *The Home* [New York: McClure, Phillips & Co., 1903], vii–xi)


## In Honor / Chant Royale

In Memory of Elizabeth Cady Stanton[23] and Cornelia D. Hussey[24]

From that dim past where clouds of darkness lower,
    Weary the steps of our long wandering;
Slow grew the savage to his human power,
    Slow came the freedom we so proudly sing.
    Far have we grown; no more we bow the knee
    To kings or idols. Partly we are free;
For in all ages some strong being rose.
Brain that can think; heart that no terror knows,
    Ears that can hear and eyes that are not blind.
All love, all rev'rence, the present owes
    In honor of the helpers of mankind.

Long were men serfs, black was their bread and sour:
    Weary their yoke and sore the lash's sting:
No more to feudal lord need vassal cower,
    Free are men now after long suffering
    Men have established widening victory
    Over the fruitful land and restless sea.
Men have long mastered their primeval foes,
And each swift century new conquest shows.
    Won by the few, with gains for all to find;
So moves the world, till every true heart glows,
    In honor of the helpers of mankind.

But woman! Hardly from the dawning hour
    Of history has she been free to fling
Apart the doors of hovel or of bower,
    And take her place in life's long forward swing.
    Free for all growth and upward progress he,
    Held to the grade of life's beginnings she.

Helplessly reaping what he broadcast sows,
       Bound in the world where he so freely goes.
Imprisoned where he fondly says "enshrined,"
       Praise to their names who lighten woman's woes.
In honor of the helpers of mankind.

At last the woman's age. At last the flower
       Of the long seed time. Far and wide doth ring
The cry for woman's freedom. Time's rich dower
       Has crowded our century with a brilliant string
       Of splendid names the future long will see
       With pride and love. Grateful and proud are we
For our great leader, who in trenchant prose
And word and thought free as the wind that blows
       Woke the world's heart and roused the slumbering mind.
Fame on her grave undying laurels strews
       In honor of the helpers of mankind.

And can none help save those who shine and tower
       High over all? Is there no offering
Gladdening and fruitful as the summer shower
       Which other souls which long to serve may bring?
For one who speaks with tongue or pen must be
       A thousand who would help us joyfully
In other ways. Give praise to one of these,
To one whose wealth still generously outflows
       To help us all. The noble heart inclined
To serve, will serve. Let us her name enclose
       In honor of the helpers of mankind.

       Envoy
Women! who see the light a great life throws
Across our darkness—a light that grows and grows:
       Let us, too, help the world, as God designed,
With broad devotion, that each soul bestows
       In honor of the helpers of mankind!
              (*Woman's Journal*, 28 March 1903, 97)


## A Glimpse of New Orleans / Triolet

       A city of gardens fair
And homes serene and stately;
       A soft, entrancing air,
       A city of gardens fair,
       And a brave new spirit there
That has come to the world but lately;
       A city of gardens fair
And homes serene and stately.
              (*Woman's Journal*, 18 April 1903, 121)

## For This New Year

As human creatures in a human world
    What should we pray?
To be more human for each others' sake,
To make ourselves more human, and help make
    The world that way.

As woman creatures in a woman's world,
    What should we give?
Give mother love to every baby there,
Protection, and true teaching, and right care,
    To all who live.

As women in a world of warring men,
    What should be do?
Prove in achievement, wisdom, love and power,
Claim and fulfil the duty of the hour—
    Prove the claim true.

As housekeepers and servants of the house,
    What do we need?
To learn a truth all human life has shown—
No woman liveth to herself along—
    Can so succeed.

As members of one vital growing race,
    What is our part?
To feel the common power, the common pride,
The common love and joy, that fill so wide
    The human heart.
        (*Woman's Journal*, 2 January 1904, 2)


## The Clam and the Lark

"I am happy," said the clam,
    "I can suck!
Sitting softly, sinking slowly
    In the muck.
I am very fat and well—
Nothing hurts me—see my shell!
    Nothing worries me at all;
Simple is the world, and small;
And I've not a thing to do
Save to let the dirt run through.
    Other people seek and strive—
    I am glad to be alive.
They'd have dinner free and fine
Had they simple tastes like mine.

There's no end of pleasant muck—
    I can suck."

"I am happy," said the lark,
    "I can sing!
Rising swiftly, rising strongly
    On the wing.
Thank the Lord for food and rest,
For the safe and dainty nest,
    For the little brood below
    And sweet wife who loves me so!
Thank Him more that I can see,
Beyond all that comes to me,
    Flower-gemmed earth so warm and fair,
    The gold sunshine and blue air!
Thank Him most for heights unending
And the glory of ascending!
    Thank the lord for power of wing
    And power to sing!"
        (*Woman's Journal*, 9 January 1904, 10)

## Coming

Because the time is ripe, the age is ready,
Because the world her woman's help demands,
Out of the long subjection and seclusion
Come to our field of warfare and confusion
The mother's heart and hands.

Long has she stood aside, endured and waited,
While man swung forward, toiling on alone;
Now, for the weary man, so long ill-mated,
Now, for the world for which she was created,
Comes woman to her own.

Not for herself! though sweet the air of freedom;
Not for herself! though dear the new-born power;
But for the child, who needs a nobler mother,
For the whole people, needing one another,
Comes woman to her hour.
        (*Woman's Journal*, 16 January 1904, 18)

## The "Old" Woman

Don't talk to me of modern wives—
"Advanced," "progressive," "new"—
And the dreadful "coming woman"
    So forced upon my view!

I'd rather look the other way,
    Through soft romantic shades,
To the mediæval lady
    Among her sewing maids.

It minds me of those feudal days
    Of mirth and minstrelsy,
When I kept a private Bard to praise
    The noble deeds of me.

When I led a band of private men,
    Retainers brave and cool,
And maintained with laugh and largesse
    My wholly private Fool.

I've lost my bard, I've lost my sword!
    I've lost baronial life!
There's nothing left of the feudal lord
    Except his feudal wife!

I love to see her so remain
    Through motionless decades
Striving in vain to still maintain
    Those feudal sewing maids.

Still further do I love to look
    Down all the line of life,
Past every step of progress to
    My Paleolithic wife!

Dear woman! Doing all her work
    At our domestic shrine—
How it brings back those early days
    When I was doing mine!

When slow I chipped the arrowhead,
    And swift I chased the bear;
And with my own two hands won all
    We had to eat and wear.

I was the happiest of men
    In those dear days of stone;
My family had but little, but
    It came from me alone.

Now they are housed and clothed and fed
    By a thousand men to-day;
But it's better to have women work
    In the sweet primeval way.

Give us united fatherhood,
    All organized and free

But a protosocial mother
        In domestic industry!

This new advance of woman
        The normal husband fears—
We'd rather have our wives behind
        By several thousand years.
                (*Woman's Journal*, 23 January 1904, 26)

## A Valentine to the Bluestocking

Lady whose pen is a power!
        Lady of brilliance and brain!
Low at thy footstool I cower,
        Humblest of all in thy train,
        Secure and serene in thy reign,
Unapproachable, high and apart
        Speak! May thy servant remain?
Tell me—hast thou a heart?

Cometh there never an hour
        That wearies of glory and gain?
When gold in a Danæan shower[25]
        Seems only a weight and a chain?
        When thou longest no more to attain
Success in the temple, the mart,
        With the restless wild effort and strain,
Tell me—hast thou a heart?

So proud in thy beautiful bower!
        So strong with thy art to sustain.
Thinkest thou ne'er that the flower
        Or thy youth may yet wither and wane?
        Of the joys that a home would contain?
Alone with thy pride and thy art
        Love's messengers woo thee in vain.
Tell me—hast thou a heart?
                Envoy.
        Star by whose beams I am slain!
            Slain as a deer by a dart!
        Speak! If thou pitiest pain,
            Tell me—hast thou a heart?
                (*Woman's Journal*, 13 February 1904, 50)

## Her Answer

Have I a heart? and pray why should you doubt it?
Think you a woman ever lived without it?
And why should I, in artificial rhymes,

Outworn pretence of mediæval times,
Come questioning of the woman of to-day
As to her heart! Why should she turn to say
To you, or such as you, that being human
In work and freedom, makes her no less woman.
A woman, with a heart. She did not choose it,
But, being born therewith, should learn to use it.
And she is learning, in these later days,
To use her heart in larger, lovelier ways;
To love not those who cringe and praise and doubt her.
But the whole aching hungry world about her.
And love means labor. Do you think her pen
Seeks but for fame and money? Here again
Speaks the mean mind. Can life be satisfied
Merely to eat and love—without the wide
Sweet glory of expression? To work well
Is duty and best pleasure. Hearts that swell
With tender triumph in good service done
Can answer you—I hope I too have one.
Yet, further, why assume I live alone?
Cold, proud, companionless, till youth be flown?
Be now informed. I have a much-prized home;
There children to my happy arms have come,
And one love reigns forever there—strong, true—
I have a heart—but it is not for you!
(Woman's Journal, 13 February 1904, 50)


## My Lady's Hat / A Pantun

How wonderful my lady's hat!
    I view it with sincere amaze.
Marvelling inwardly thereat
    Whenever it affronts my gaze.

I view it with sincere amaze;
    How it doth spread like angel's wings,
Whenever it attracts my gaze,
    Extinguishing all other things!

How it doth spread like angel's wings.
    How it obtrudes, and hides from view
(Extinguishing all other things)
    The loveliness I thought I knew!

How it obtrudes, and hides from view
    Her unforgettable fair face!
The loveliness I thought I knew
    Would gladden me in any place.

Her unforgettable fair face,
    Her winding harmony of hair,
Would gladden me in any place,
    If she would only bring them there—

Her winding harmony of hair
    Where loving thought is softly led—
If she would only bring them there—
    Without this insult overhead—

Where loving thought is softly led
    To dwell on beauty, love and youth,
Without this insult overhead—
    A sneer for art, a scorn for truth.

To dwell on beauty, love and youth,
    We lean our hearts with reverence fit;
A sneer for art, a scorn for truth,
    She gives us in the place of it.

We lean our hearts with reverence fit
    To beauty, crowned, intelligent,
She gives to us in place of it
    This lunacy of ornament.

To beauty, crowned, intelligent,
    The world does homage from its heart.
This lunacy of ornament
    Is neither nature nor yet art.

The world does homage from its heart
    To beauty, heaven's perfect way.
Is neither nature nor yet art
    Worthy a woman's thought to-day?

To beauty, heaven's perfect way,
    These towering discords never lead;
Worthy a woman's thought to-day
    Is the far sequence of her deed.

These towering discords never lead
    Man from the place he holds behind.
Is the far sequence of her deed
    Production of degenerate mind?

Man, from the place he holds behind,
    Marveling inwardly thereat;
Production of degenerate mind—
    How wonderful my lady's hat!
      (*Twentieth-Century Home*, 1 [March 1904], 43)

## The Purpose

Serene she sat, full grown in human power,
Established in the service of the world,
Full-hearted, rich, strong with the age's life,
Wise with the womanhood of centuries,
With broad still brown and deep eyes lit beneath
With fire of inextinguishable love,
In beauty which the study of a life
Would fail to measure—beauty as of hills
Or the heart-stilling wonder of the sea.

Then came her lovers, awed and passionate,
With naught to offer that she had not more
Save only—manhood. Lovers made by God
To order to her final power of choice
Their natural tribute of diverging gifts,
The man's inherent variance of growth,
That she, by choosing, build a better race.
Theirs the resistless longing to fulfill
Their nature's primal law at any cost,
The one great purpose of their parted life;
Love their first cause, love their determined end.

So she, from ardent emulous appeal,
After the inner ruling of her heart
Chose him of all best mated to herself,
Best qualified to glorify The Child—
For this was she made woman—not for him.
(*Woman's Journal*, 12 March 1904, 82)


## Missing the Way

It is so dark! I must have lost my way!
    It is so difficult and strange and steep—
    Rock upon rock, rank marsh, black waters deep—
Far from the path that should have been I stray.

No, friend, not lost at all—this is the way.
    It's not all pleasant, we are quite aware,
    But most of us, just now must travel alone,
And our worst trouble is the fear to stray.

In blessed truth we cannot really stray;
    Whatever comes is Life; and the strong soul
    Finds in its living a continued goal—
All makes for growing—growing is the way.
(*Woman's Journal*, 26 March 1904, 98)

## Human Living

Living is doing: Doing the deeds that are human;
Not merely the functions of man or the function of woman,
But the later and larger work of our nobler order,
Work that is measure of progress—Time's recorder;
Connected, specialized, wide in fluent relation,
Distinguishing man from man—knitting nation to nation.

Living is power's discharge: The world's force splendid
Pouring, from year to year, through our work unended;
Growing from hour to hour as our work is truer,
Richer and fuller fruit of the joyous doer.
Not for ourselves! the beast may be self-sustaining,
But we support one another in boundless gaining.

Still we must eat and sleep, and make more people?
True; but it needs no preaching under a steeple;
True, for us and the beast, a law there is no unloosing;
Duty of eating and sleeping and cleaning and reproducing;
Law of the animal world under nature's giving—
The basis and background of life—but it is not living!
                    (*Woman's Journal*, 2 April 1904, 106)


## What Counts

You may stuff your brain till it jumps the pan,
 Like over-risen dough,
But you'll never be a better man
 Till you do the things you know.

You may feel your love go round the earth,
 As a tire goes around a wheel,
But the world will never know its worth
 Till you do the things you feel.

Your head may be lord over all the land—
 Your heart may deserve a crown—
But it's what you do with your actual hands
 That keeps the whole world down.

Men know the ties of our human life,
 And feel its mutual law,
But they do as they did in the brute's lone strife,
 In the reign of tooth and claw.[26]

And women? We know that the world is one,
 We feel its common heart,
But we do our life-long work alone
 And hold the world apart.
                    (*Woman's Journal*, 16 April 1904, 122)

## Step by Step

Step by step you told me was the journey—
    Day after day you told me was the year—
Patience, Faith and Duty! I believed and I obeyed you;
    Centuries have rolled over me—left me here.

Life whirls by in splendid new occasions,
    Time swings on, with triumph in its train,
The world does move! Life is growth and motion!
    While I sit still, in patience, faith and pain.

I have step-by-stepped like a blind horse in a treadmill,
    I have day-after-dayed through an endless inch-worm age;
Rebellions lift the peoples—discovery! invention!
    Divine is discontent! there is righteousness in rage!

I have done with patience! I will dictate duty!
    Child of mine no more shall hear what I have borne so long!
Foresight, effort, daring, shall guide to ease and beauty,
    And show my crippled sisters that their petty rules are wrong.
    (*Woman's Journal*, 30 April 1904, 138)

## "O 'Tis Love, 'Tis Love, 'Tis Love That Makes the World Go Round"[27]

Why should the people of to-day
Believe the things old poets say
    As if all tales were true—
    As if those people knew?
Because our ancestors were sold,
Believing all that they were told,
    That isn't proof, you know—
    That doesn't make it so!

We love in France, we love in Spain,
Across the world and back again
    We're loving with a will;
But some live nations forge ahead
Some drop behind, as good as dead.
    And some are sitting still.

Did love propel Columbus' keel?[28]
Make Darwin[29] think or Froebel[30] feel?
    Still oil, develop coal?
Was Watt[31] in love when watching steam?
Is railroad conquest Love's young dream?
    Does Eros seek the pole?

O bless you, no! They love in Hindustan:[32]
But precious slow those people go

In spite of Cupid's plan.
The Roman ringed the world with power,
The Turk and Tartar had their hour,
    The Hindu also ran.

They love in China, too, but what does China do?
    For all her lover's sighs and tears
    She has not moved in a thousand years!
Surely enough to show Love doesn't make us go!
Because a thing is said and said,
By many living and more dead,
    That doesn't make it *so!*
O bless you, no!
        (*Woman's Journal*, 7 May 1904, 146)

## Faith and Fact

Have you lost your hold on God?
Fallen low, sunk again,
Into error, weakness, pain,
Till the light no more seems true.
Fear not in the dark and cold;
God has never lost his hold
    Upon you.

Have you lost your faith in God?
Learned too much, grown too wise
To believe mistakes and lies?
Still the Primal Force doth act,
Fear not in the light to-day;
Better than all faith can say
    Is the fact.
        (*Woman's Journal*, 21 May 1904, 162)

## Where We Leave Off

Where we leave off and something else begins—
Not at our skins,
Not at the garments new
With which we cover them:
Not at the door-step, nor the dooryard fence,
Nor where the city dense
Thins gradually to the open land;
Not at the strand
Of this our country, where the surf-beat dies,
Or map-line lies:
Not with the hemisphere!—the human soul
Needs the world whole.

The human spirit dwells
Not only in the tongue that tells
Of love, the eye we look through, or the hand;
We've more than flesh at our command;
The ax alone
Is nearer human than our flesh and bone.
The spade, the plow, the knife—slow social laws
Evolved us there—our human teeth and claws
Where speaks the organ or the violin—we dwell therein.
Huge engines toll for us in silent ease—we are in these.
The human body, grown from hand and brain—
In it we grow again.

(*Woman's Journal*, 4 June 1904, 178)

## Pushing into the Days

Pushing into the days—
The little dark days that crowd so fast;
Pushing the small days steadily on—
This and that, with a careful hand,
Quiet, unhurried, all of it counts.
Stopping to drink at the evening's end,—
Beginning the day with a long, deep draught,
Of the whole great purpose slow
The whole—which we may not hope to see
While we take hold of the present part—
Yet part by part must the whole be won.

(*Woman's Journal*, 11 June 1904, 186)

## For Each Day

For each day
To pray
New hold, new touch, to feel
The swift broad current of the world's great life;
And so,
Letting power out, to grow
Ever the stronger. Smooth the living
That feels the endless income smoothly flow,
And pours as smoothly—giving, giving, giving.

(*Woman's Journal*, 18 June 1904, 194)

## Strange Lands

Of all strange lands whose luring charms we own,
Full of new knowledge and wind wonder sweet,

None is more darkly, utterly unknown
    Than the long-trodden fields beneath our feet.

Of all strange powers wherewith the soul holds sway,
    Is none more starkly marvelous than this:
Itself can push its dearest faiths away
    For one strong moment—and behold what is!
      (*Cosmopolitan*, 37 [July 1904], 338)

## Climb a Tree

Look ahead! look ahead! as far as you can see!
You can never find the pass
With your eyes among the grass;
If the bushes hide and hinder—
    Climb a tree!

Here you are, born and reared—this they call "your lot"
It would seem, to hear their talk,
You were a cabbage stalk.
Shake a leg, my friend, and show them
    That you're not!

You can move! you can rise! you're alive and free!
Get on somewhere every day,
And, when you can't see the way,
Don't run round in treadmill circles—
    Climb a tree!
      (*Woman's Journal*, 13 August 1904, 258)

## Human Pain

A world of joy! a world of light!
    A world of wealth we own!
Yet we sit sad and dim of sight,
Starving and waiting in the night
    Each is a hole alone.

We feel the ache of the brutal past
    From age to age again;
Heard it and nurse and make it last,
Teach it, reform it, and hold it fast—
    And we call it Human Pain!

Ache of the heart for its food denied,
    Or the mate it could not gain;
Ache for the young that was born and cried,
For the helpless young that helpless died—
    That is not *Human* Pain!

Human pain is a splendid thing,
    The throb of the great world soul,
The healthy hurt, the warning sting
That shows the wrong in suffering
    That drives to the onward goal!

But most our own is the full delight
    Of the thing we ought to be—
A joy like sunshine, wide and bright,
That is the Human creature's right—
    Not this brute agony!
        (*Woman's Journal*, 27 August 1904, 274)


## Heirlooms

To my child I have transmitted,
    Just as they were given me,
The traditions that were fitted
To my ancient feeble-witted
    Undeveloped ancestry.

Sacred feeling, pure emotions,
    Which originally came
From the age of lukewarm oceans
And vast beasts of sinuous motions—
    And were suited to the same.

All untouched the gift has rested—
    I have never cut the string—
Unassorted, undigested,
Unconsidered, uncontested—
    Take, my child, the sacred thing!

But presume not to unfold it:
    Let no worn-out remnant stray—
Just exactly as you hold it
Let more ages harder mould it—
    Hand it down along the way.
        (*Woman's Journal*, 3 September 1904, 282)


## Labor is Prayer

What should I ask of God?
To come? He is here.
He is here and now in me. It is Him that I feel.
I, feeling, am that much God.
To give? He has given, is giving, gives.
The flow and the pulse of things,
Each step and quiver of life, is full of God.

Should an egg pray to be given? Nay, to be hatched.
And will hatch, pray or not, if alive.
If it were ready, willing, only the shell not broken,
It had better peek than be praying.
What should I ask of God?
God, who pushes and pushes
With the tides of the whole creation.
He might ask me for something—
Namely, to get a move on—
To let Him through and not hinder!
God is not slow nor deficient.
He does not need a reminder.
He is strictly attending to business.
Still, things don't work as they ought to—
Something does ail the procession—
It wavers, sticks and drops backward.
Well, what ails the procession?
Some men stopping and waiting,
Some men wriggling backwards,
And praying—or urging to praying—
That God will move the procession!
Would you be wound up like a puppet?
Marionettes of High Heaven?
Or like a recalcitrant baby,
Dragged by the arms—heels rebellious!
Pray to yourself—that you travel!
Or,—without praying—just travel!
(*Out West*, 22 [May 1905], 407)


## Freedom

Only in freedom are great virtues found
    And grown to greater heights; for in the slave
    Is neither the strong courage of the brave,
Nor honor, by whose code the brave are bound;
Not that great glory, justice, loftiest crowned,
    Nor truth—the light that God to nature gave;
    Not even the pure fire of loving—save—
The blind subservient loving of the hound.
No praise, no pride, no privilege, atone
    For liberty denied. For that one thing
    Uncounted lives have poured, in purchasing
Even the poor half-freedom we have known.
    No freedom worth the name the world can see
    Till woman, the world-mother, is made free.
(*Woman's Journal*, 15 July 1905, 109)

## The Little White Animals

We who have grown human—house-bodied, cloth-skinned,
Wire-nerved and steam-hearted—alas! we forget
The poor little beasts we have bandaged and pinned
And hid in our carpet-lined prisons!—and yet
Though our great social body be brickwork and steel,
The little white animals in it, can feel!

Humanity needs them. We cannot disclaim
The laws of the bodies we lived in before
We grew to be human. In spite of our frame
Of time-scorning metals, the life at its core,
Controlling its action and guarding its ease,
Is the little white animal out of the trees!

It is true that our soul is far higher than theirs;
We look farther, live longer, love wider—we *know*;
They only can feel, for themselves, and their heirs;
We, the life of humanity. Yet, even so,
We must always remember that soul at its base
Looks out through the little white animal's face.

If they die we are dead. If they live we can grow.
They ply in our streets as blood corpuscles ply
In their own little veins. If you cut off the flow
Of these beasts in a city, that city will die.
Yet we heighten our buildings and harden our souls
Till the little white animals perish in shoals.

Their innocent instincts we turn to a curse,
Their bodies we torture, their powers we abuse;
The beast that humanity lives in fares worse
Than the beasts of the forest with nothing to lose;
Free creatures, sub-human:—they never have known
The sins and diseases we force on our own.

And yet 'tis a beautiful creature!—tall—fair—
With features full pleasant and hand-wooing hair;
Kind, docile, intelligent, eager to learn;
And the longing we read in its eyes when they burn
Is to beg us to use it more freely to show
To each other the love that our new soul can know.

Our engines drive fast in earth, water and air
Our resistless, smooth-running machines still unroll,
With brainwork unceasing and handiwork fair,
New material forms for each step of the soul:
But that soul, for the contact without which it dies,
Comes closest of all through that animal's eyes.

(*Conservator*, 18 [October 1907], 116)

## There is No Payment

Brother—there is no payment in the world!
We work and pour our labor at the feet
Of those who are around us and to come.
We live and take our living at the hands
Of those who are around us and have been.
No one is paid. No person can have more
Than he can hold. And none can do beyond
The power that's in him. To each child that's born
Belongs as much of all our human good
As he can take and use to make him strong.
And from each man, debtor to all the world,
Is due the fullest fruit of all his powers,
His whole life's labor, proudly rendered up
Not as return—can moments pay and age?
But as the simple duty of a man.
Can he do less—receiving everything?
　　　　(*Friends' Intelligencer*, 25 January 1908: 65)


## To the Wise—A Bargain

Said the Slumchild to the Wise—
To the people of place and power
Who govern and guide the hour,
To the people who write and teach,
Ruling our thought and speech,
And all the Captains and Kings
Who command the making of things:—
"Give me the good ye know,
That I, the child, my grow!
Light, for the whole day long,
Food that is pure and strong,
Housing and clothing fair,
Clean water and clean air,
Teaching them from day to day,
And room—for a child to play!"

Then the wise made answer cold;
"These things are not given, but sold.
They shall be yours today
　　　If you can pay."

"Pay!" said the child, "Pay you!
What can I do?
Only in years' slow length
Shall I have strength.
I have not power nor skill,

Wisdom nor wit nor will—
What services weak and wild
Can you ask of a little child?"

But the wise made answer cold:
"Goods must be bought and sold;
You shall have nothing here
Without paying—paying dear!"
And the Rulers turned away,
But the child cried to them: "Stay!
 Wait! I will pay!"

"For the foulness where I live,
Filth in return I give.
For the greed that withholds my right,
Greed that shall shake your might,
For the sins I live in and learn,
Plentiful sin I return
For my lack in home and school,
Ignorance comes to rule.
From where I sicken and die,
Disease in your homes shall lie.
My all uncounted death
Shall choke your children's breath.
Degenerate—crippled—base
I degrade the human race;
And the people you have made—
These shall make you afraid.
I ask no more. I take
The terms you make;
And steadily, day by day,
 I will pay."
   (*Public*, 22 February 1908, 1116)


## Song for Equal Suffrage

Day of hope and day of glory! After slavery and woe,
Comes the dawn of woman's freedom, and the light shall grow and grow
Until every man and woman equal liberty shall know,
 In Freedom marching on!

Woman's right is woman's duty! For our share in life we call!
Our will it is not weakened and our power it is not small.
We are half of every nation! We are mothers of them all!
 In Wisdom marching on!

Not for self but larger service has our cry for freedom grown,
There is crime, disease and warfare in a world of men alone,

In the name of love we're rising now to serve and save our own,
  As Peace comes marching on!

By every sweet and tender tie around our heartstrings curled,
In the cause of nobler motherhood is woman's flag unfurled,
Till every child shall know the joy and peace of mother's world—
  As Love comes marching on!

We will help to make a pruning hook of every outgrown sword,
We will help to knit the nations in continuing accord,
In humanity made perfect is the glory of the Lord,
  As His world goes marching on!
      (*Woman's Journal*, 13 February 1909, 28)


## Water-lilies

I shall have water-lilies then—
White—white as daylight,
Sweet warm gold at heart,
With all cool green in their soft leaves and stems
And flush of rose, deep rose, along the buds.
Flowers should give beauty. Here is beauty, full,
Flowers should give fragrance. These have breath so sweet
One drowses with wide arms and dreams of love;
Flowers should suggest surrounding loveliness;—
And these? Beside sweet odor and white grace
These fill the soul with memories of joy
In water, quiet water dark and cool.
Slow rivers stealing by the velvet rim
Where largest violets with long white stems
Stand in the tender grass. Brown pools—
Clear, clear as glass, with green leaves overhead,
And dark mosaic floor of leaves below.
And lakes, blue lakes, broad-bosomed, swept by winds;
Small lakes, deep-shaded, silent, dimly green;
And the still lily-ponds—so thick with these!
      (*Harper's Bazaar*, 43 [September 1909], 887)


## 13 Epigraphs to *What Diantha Did*[33]

I
One may use the Old Man of the Sea,
    For a partner or patron,
  But helpless and hapless is he
  Who is ridden, inextricably,
      By a fond old mer-matron.

II

The brooding bird fulfills her task,
      Or she-bear lean and brown;
  All parent beasts see duty true,
  All parent beasts their duty do,
  We are the only kind that asks
      For duty upside down.

III

Duck! Dive! Here comes another one!
  Wait till the crest-ruffles show!
  Beyond is smooth water in beauty and wonder—
  Shut your mouth!  Hold your breath!  Dip your head under!
  Dive through the weight and the wash, and the thunder—
  Look out for the undertow!

IV

"Lovest thou me?" said the Fair Ladye;
      And the Lover he said, "Yea!"
  "Then climb this tree—for my sake," said she,
      "And climb it every day!"
  So from dawn till dark he abrazed the bark
      And wore his clothes away;
  Till, "What has this tree to do with thee?"
      The Lover at last did say.

V

When the fig grows on the thistle,
And the silk purse on the sow;
When one swallow brings the summer,
And blue moons on her brow—

Then we may look for strength and skill,
Experience, good health, good will,
Art and science well combined,
Honest soul and able mind,
Servants built upon this plan,
One to wait on every man,
Patiently from youth to age,—
For less than a street cleaner's wage!

When the parson's gay on Mondays,
When we meet a month of Sundays,
We may look for them and find them—
      But Not Now!

VI

It's a singular thing that the commonest place
  Is the hardest to properly fill;
That the labor imposed on a full half the race

Is so seldom performed with good will—
To say nothing of knowledge or skill!

What we ask of all women, we stare at in one,
    And tribute of wonderment bring;
If this task of the million is once fitly done
    We all hold our hands up and sing!
    It's really a singular thing!

VII

You may talk about religion with a free and open mind,
        For ten dollars you may criticize a judge;
    You may discuss in politics the newest thing you find,
        And open scientific truth to all the deaf and blind,
    But there's one place where the brain must never budge!
CHORUS.
    Oh, the Home is Utterly Perfect!
    And all its works within!
        To say a word about it—
        To criticize or doubt it—
        To seek to mend or move it—
        To venture to improve it—
    Is The Unpardonable Sin!
                —"Old Song."

VIII

She beats upon her bolted door,
    With faint weak hands;
Drearily walks the narrow floor;
Sullenly sits, blank walls before;
    Despairing stands.

Life calls her, Duty, Pleasure, Gain—
    Her dreams respond;
But the blank daylights wax and wane,
Dull peace, sharp agony, slow pain—
    No hope beyond.

Till comes a thought! She lifts her head,
    The world grows wide!
A voice—as if clear words were said—
"Your door, so long imprisoned,
    Is locked inside!"

IX

Men have marched in armies, fleets have borne them,
    Left their homes new countries to subdue;
Young men seeking fortune wide have wandered—
    We have something new.

Armies of young maidens cross our oceans;
     Leave their mother's love, their father's care;
Maidens, young and helpless, widely wander,
     Burdens new to bear.

Strange the land and language, laws and customs;
     Ignorant and all alone they come;
Maidens young and helpless, serving strangers,
     Thus we keep The Home.

When on earth was safety for young maidens
     Far from mother's love and father's care?
We preserve The Home, and call it sacred—
     Burdens new they bear.

X

"We are weak!" said the Sticks, and men broke them;
     "We are weak!" said the Threads, and were torn;
Till new thoughts came and they spoke them;
     Till the Fagot and the Rope were born.

For the Fagot men find is resistant,
     And they anchor on the Rope's taut length;
Even grasshoppers combined,
     Are a force, the farmers find—
In union there is strength.

XI

Your car is too big for one person to stir—
     Your chauffeur is a little man, too;
Yet he lifts that machine, does the little chauffeur,
     By the power of a gentle jackscrew.

XII

The Earth-plants spring up from beneath,
     The Air-plants swing down from above,
          But the Banyan trees grow
          Both above and below,
     And one makes a prosperous grove.

XIII

They laid before her conquering feet
     The spoils of many lands;
Their crowns shone red upon her head
     Their scepters in her hands.

She heard two murmuring at night,
     Where rose-sweet shadows rest;
And coveted the blossom red
     He laid upon her breast.

          (from *What Diantha Did* [New York: Charlton, 1910], *passim*)

## 13 Epigraphs to *The Crux*[34]

Who should know but the woman?—The young wife-to-be?
    Whose whole life hangs on the choice;
To her the ruin, the misery;
    To her, the deciding voice.

Who should know but the woman?—The mother-to-be?
    Guardian, Giver, and Guide;
If she may not foreknow, forejudge and foresee,
    What safety has childhood beside?

Who should know but the woman?—The girl in her youth?
    The hour of the warning is then,
That, strong in her knowledge and free in her truth,
    She may build a new race of men.

I
Along the same old garden path,
Sweet with the same old flowers;
Under the lilacs, darkly dense,
The easy gate in the backyard fence—
Those unforgotten hours!

II
Lockstep, handcuffs, ankle-ball-and-chain,
Dull toil and dreary food and drink;
Small cell, cold cell, narrow bed and hard;
High wall, thick wall, window iron-barred;
Stone-paved, stone-pent little prison yard—
Young hearts weary of monotony and pain,
Young hearts weary of reiterant refrain:
"They say—they do—what will people think?"

III
There comes a time
After white months of ice—

Slow months of ice—long months of ice—
There comes a time when the still floods below
Rise, lift, and overflow—
Fast, far they go.

IV
Sometimes a plant in its own habitat
    Is overcrowded, starved, oppressed and daunted;
A palely feeble thing; yet rises quickly,
    Growing in height and vigor, blooming thickly,
        When far transplanted.

V

Old England thinks our country
    Is a wilderness at best—
And small New England thinks the same
    Of the large free-minded West.

Some people know the good old way
    Is the only way to do,
And find there must be something wrong
    In anything that's new.

VI

'Twould be too bad to be true, my dear,
    And wonders never cease;
'Twould be too bad to be true, my dear,
    If all one's swans were geese.

VII

High shines the golden shield in front,
    To those who are not blind;
      And clear and bright
      In all men's sight,
    The silver shield behind.

In breadth and sheen each face is seen;
    How tall it is, how wide;
      But its thinness shows
      To only those
    Who stand on either side.

VIII

In poetry and painting and fiction we see
    Such praise for the Dawn of the Day,
We've long since been convinced that a sunrise must be
    All Glorious and Golden and Gay.

But we find there are mornings quite foggy and drear,
    With the clouds in a low-hanging pall;
Till the grey light of daylight can hardly make clear
    That the sun has arisen at all.

IX

You may have a fondness for grapes that are green,
And the sourness that greenness beneath;
    You may have a right
    To a colic at night—
But consider your children's teeth!

X

You may shut your eyes with a bandage,
    The whole world vanishes soon;

You may open your eyes at a knothole
    And see the sun and moon.

XI

If I do right, though heavens fall,
    And end all light and laughter;
Though black the night and ages long,
    Bitter the cold—the tempest strong—
If I do right, and brave it all—
    The sun shall rise thereafter!

XII

There are some folks born to beauty,
    And some to plenteous gold,
Some who are proud of being young,
    Some proud of being old.

Some who are glad of happy love,
    Enduring, deep and true,
And some who thoroughly enjoy
    The little things they do.
        (from *The Crux* [New York: Charlton, 1911], *passim*)

## ["'Ah, who am I that God should bow]

"'Ah, who am I that God should bow
    From heaven to choose a wife for me?
What have I done He should endow
    My home with thee?'"
        (from *The Crux* [New York: Charlton, 1911], 182)

## We Stand as One

Air: Kathleen Aroon[35]

Long have we lived apart,
    Women alone;
Each with an empty heart,
    Women alone;
Now we begin to see
How to live safe and free,
No more on earth shall be
    Women alone.

Now we have learned the truth,
    Union is power;
Weak and strong, age and youth,
    Union is power;
On to the end we go,

Stronger our League must grow,
We can win Justice so,
    Union is power!

For the right pay for us,
    We stand as one;
For the short day for us,
    We stand as one;
Loyal and brave and strong,
Helping the world along,
For end to every wrong
    We stand as one!
        (*Life and Labor*, 2 [May 1912], 153)


## Womanhood

We fear, while old walls break and old bonds sever,
    Lest we lose Life's most precious things forever—
Heart jewels, valued all the world above.
    We fear the loss of Womanhood—no other;
    With Man's dear temple, Home; his idol, Mother;
His dream, hope, comfort, spur and blessing—Love.

We need not fear. While our life shall endure,
Woman with man remaineth, steadfast, sure;
And Womanhood means Mother, Home and Love.
    (*Delineator*, 85 [December 1914], 5)


## Wouldn't You Think?

Wouldn't you think, if it is right to seize
    A man, and hide him in a pile of stone,
Rob him of sunshine, starlight, grass and trees,
    Freedom and friendship; bottle him, alone,
An Amputated Man—as where one sees
    A finger in formaldehyde, to show
The horrible result of some disease—
    Wouldn't you think—if 'tis right, you know—
Society, to take such vengeance strong,
Must blame and fear, in him some awful wrong?

Wouldn't you think, if any little child,
    Born a pink baby, wholly innocent,
May grow up dissolute, fierce, tempered, wild
    Of mischievous behavior and intent;
If, out of infancy so undefiled,
    May grow a criminal, of sins so great
As warrants cruelty or vengeance piled;
    Wouldn't you think, if crime so hurts the State,

That State would guard the baby unafraid,
And see that no more criminals were made?

Wouldn't you think, since prisons cost so dear;
    Since keeping prisoners all the guards degrade;
Since men imprisoned leave all poorer here
    For lack of each man's service in his trade,
Since prisoners' families the wolf must fear,
    Or tax the State as our tax-payers know;
Since long the lists of legal costs appear;
    Wouldn't you think—if all these things are so—
Society would find it less a curse
To make men better than to make them worse?
       (*Survey*, 22 April 1916, 101)

## Woman's Hour

Not for herself! Though sweet the air of freedom;
Not for herself! Though dear for the new-born power;
But for the Child who needs a nobler Mother,
For the Whole People needing One Another,
Comes Woman to her Hour.
       (*Woman's Journal*, 9 December 1916, 397)

## Two

Man the hunter, Man the warrior,
Slew for gain and slew for safety,
Slew for rage, for sport, for glory—
    Slaughter was his breath;
So the man's mind, searching inward,
Saw in all one red reflection,
Filled the world with dark religions
    Built on Death,

Death, and the Fate of the Soul;—
The Soul, from the body dissevered,
Through the withering failure of age,
Through the horror and pain of disease,
Through raw wounds and destruction and fear;—
In fear, black fear of the dark,
Red fear of terrible gods,
Sent forth on its journey alone,
To eternity, fearful, unknown—
    Death, and the Fate of the Soul.

Woman, bearer; Woman, teacher;
Overflowing love and labor,
Service of the tireless mother

Filling all the earth;—
Now her mind awakening, searching,
Sees a fair world young and growing,
Sees at last our real religion—
    Built on Birth.

Birth, and the Growth of the Soul;—
The Soul, in the body established,
In the ever-new beauty of childhood,
In the wonder of opening power,
Still learning, improving, achieving,
In hope, new knowledge, and light,
Sure faith in the world's fresh Spring,—
Together we live, we grow,
On the earth that we love and know—
    Birth, and the Growth of the Soul.
        (from *His Religion and Hers* [New York: Century, 1923], n.p.)


## The Primal Power

Would ye plant the earth with new-made men?
    A race new-born, a race unstained?
Clothed in flesh that hath no flaw,
One with nature, one with law,
    Strong-souled, clear-brained?

This may motherhood achieve,
    Full-grown mothers brave and free,
Splendid bodies trained and strong,
Hearts that ache for human wrong,
    Eyes that can see.

Learning new their primal power,
    A reign forgot, a crown disowned;
Rising from their prison blind,
Pets and servants of mankind,
    Re-born, re-throned.

Theirs the power beyond appeal
    To choose the good, reject the base;
So shall all degenerate blood
Die, forbidden fatherhood—
    So rise our race!
        (from *His Religion and Hers* [New York: Century, 1923], 96–97)


## [I'm not feathers, beak, and wings]

I'm not feathers, beak, and wings,
A bird that flies, a bird that sings,—
No, you have the handle wrong;

By what gifts to me belong
I am Flying, I am Song.
   (from *His Religion and Hers* [New York: Century, 1923], 100)


## Two Hundred Words

Two hundred words—a scant array
   To carry all I'd like to say
      Of gratitude and admiration
      And heartfelt warm congratulation
To greet this Golden Wedding Day.

Dear friends, for many a year are they,
   To fitly praise I see no way,
      Nor find, to own my obligation,
      Two hundred words.

Yet from her lips, in humor gay,
   Or love, or ire, less words convey
      Delight and joy or consternation;
      And from his pen—what compensation,
What piled and willing wealth can pay
   Two hundred words?
   (*A Purse of Gold: filled by the children, the grandchildren and a few of the friends of Elizabeth and Alexander Black*[36] *in commemoration of their golden wedding anniversary* (New York: privately printed, 1931), n.p.)


## A Hundred Years Hence

A hundred years hence there'll be peace in the world,
The battleships sunk and the battle flags furled.
An end to war's death and destruction intense.
The world will be wiser a hundred years hence.
A hundred years hence.

The strong and the young are the victims we slay,
The weakly and old the survivors who stay,
We ruin the race in our folly immense
The world will be wiser a hundred years hence.
A hundred years hence.

We pile up our millions with knowledge and skill
We pour out our millions to cripple and kill,
Three-fours of our tax goes to warfare's expense[37]
The world will be wiser a hundred years hence.
A hundred years hence.

An organized world keeping peace up on earth,
The people improving in wisdom and worth—
We'd start it today if we had enough sense—

Why wait for the hope of a hundred years hence.
    A hundred years hence.
    A hundred years hence.
        (Broadside published at the Ninth Conference on the Cause and Cure of
        War, 17 January 1934.)[38]


## [O rock and ice! I offered you my hand]

"O rock and ice! I offered you my hand
    I owned I loved you, dear,
You only smiled with heartless self-command
    And bade me wait a year.

"And I have waited, with an aching breast,
    While spring to summer turned;
Waited while darkly in the distant west
    The autumn sunsets burned.

"Waited until the winter came at last
    With whirling snow and rain,
Waited until the weary year was passed
    And I might ask again.

"Will you be mine? The true love on my part
    I think you well can guess,
I listen with a horror in my heart
    Lest you should answer 'Yes!'"
        (*The Living of Charlotte Perkins Gilman*, 55)


## [For this new year unknown whose steady wing]

"For this new year unknown whose steady wing
Joy, Peace or Pain may bring, I plan one thing.

"In this new year which finds me still so weak
From loss the past can speak, one thing I seek.
For one thing shall my soul's hands lift and reach,
Praying the year may teach more perfect speech.

"Clean, honest, wise, correct, strong, gentle too—
Courteous as angels, set in order due, perfectly true.
        (*The Living of Charlotte Perkins Gilman*, 135)


## [I wait the coming year too sad for fear]

"I wait the coming year too sad for fear
Too old for hope, too wise for real despair,
Wait it in patient prayer.

"It matters little about me if so I be
Able to make the effort of one soul
Help on the whole.

"Only not too much pain! Oh not again
That anguish of dead years—
Terror and tears!"
(*The Living of Charlotte Perkins Gilman*, 135–36)


## For 1899

For this New Year—and last,
Of the century nearly past—
    Help me to grow!
Help me to fill the days
With deeds of loving praise
    For the splendid truths I know.

Help me to finish clear
All claims of the old year—
    And all behind;
And to meet all duties new
With loving service due
    And a steadfast mind.

A clear and steadfast mind!
Help me, O God, to find
    Such hold on you
As may dispel disease,
That I may work in peace,
    Work deep, work true.

Slowly so long—and dark!
Down at the lowest mark—
    The light grows now!
God! I am seeking still
To learn and do your will—
    Still show me how!
(*The Living of Charlotte Perkins Gilman*, 277)


## [So proud of our grandsires are we]

So proud of our grandsires are we
Each old house wears a sign, as you see;
    If a house we have not,
    Then we label the lot,
And hang up the sign on a tree.
(*The Living of Charlotte Perkins Gilman*, 325)

## Sophia and Amelia[39]

For four and forty vanished years
    Amelia anguished all alone,
Vain were her murmurs, vain her tears!
    Still stood the soldier on the stone.

Amelia anguished all alone.
    Sophia her sister sat in state
Still stood the soldier on the stone
    Beside the awful iron gate.

Sophia her sister sat in state
    Administering justice well.
Beside the awful iron gate
    Yawning like opening to hell.

Administering justice well.
    This is the duty of the hour:
Yawning like opening to hell
    Is the prerogative of power.

This is the duty of the hour.
    Therefore Amelia has to wait.
Is the only prerogative of power
    Only to guard an iron gate?

Therefore Amelia has to wait
    Until Sophia has had her swing
Only to guard an iron gate
    This is the duty that I sing.

Until Sophia has had her swing
    The faithful soldier sits alone.
This is the duty that I sing.
    The causes poor Amelia's moan.

The faithful soldier sits alone
    For four and forty vanished years.
This causes poor Amelia's moan—
    Vain were her murmurs, vain her tears.
        (Gilman Papers, Schlesinger Library, Radcliffe Institute, folder 193)

## The Crusade Hymn[40]

Our eyes have seen the glory of the coming of the day
When all shall give their honest work and take their honest pay,
And poverty, the social Curse, be wholly swept away—
    That day is marching on!
    CHORUS
Glory, glory, hal-le-lu-jah! Glory, glory, hal-le-lu-jah!

Glory, glory, hal-le-lu-jah! That day is marching on!
We have seen it in the writing of a thousand men who know,
We have seen it in the meeting where the crowding workers go,
We have felt it in the people's heart, where all great movements grow—
      That day is marching on!
      CHORUS
The day when every man on earth shall find his fullest flower,
When Mother love shall ring the world and bring a nobler hour,
When every baby born shall live and blossom like a flower—
      That day is marching on!
      CHORUS
The end of fort and battleship! The end of gun and sword!
The end of shame and misery and vice and crime abhorred!
The time for us to build on earth the Kingdom of the Lord!
      That day is marching on!
      CHORUS
      (Gilman Papers, Schlesinger Library, Radcliffe Institute, folder 193)


## The First Idealist

A jellyfish swam in a tropical sea,
And he said, "This world it consists of me;
There's nothing above and nothing below
That a jellyfish even can possibly know
(Since we've no sight, or hearing, or smell),
Beyond what our single sense can tell
Now, all that I learn from the sense of touch
Is the fact of my feelings, viewed as such.
But to think they have any external cause
Is an inference clean against logical laws.
Again, to suppose, as I've hitherto done,
There are other jellyfish under the sun,
Is a pure assumption that can't be backed
By a jot of proof or a single fact.
In short, like Hume,[41] I very much doubt
If there's anything else at all without.
So I come at least to the plain conclusion,
When the subject is fairly set free from confusion,
That the universe simply centres in me,
And if I were not, then nothing would be."[42]
      (Gilman Papers, Schlesinger Library, Radcliffe Institute, folder 193)

# NOTES

## WORKS CITED

# NOTES

**Introduction**

1. Charlotte Perkins Gilman, *The Living of Charlotte Perkins Gilman: An Autobiography* (1935; rpt. Madison: Univ. of Wisconsin Press, 1990), 88. Hereafter, *Living.*

2. *Living*, 85.

3. Charlotte Perkins Gilman, "In Duty Bound," *Woman's Journal*, Jan. 12, 1884, 14.

4. *Living*, 91.

5. Charlotte Perkins Gilman, "The Answer," *Woman's Journal*, Oct. 2, 1886, 313.

6. *Living*, 96.

7. *Living*, 163.

8. Ibid.

9. Charlotte Perkins Gilman, "The Duty Farthest," *Impress*, Nov. 17, 1894, 5.

10. *Living*, 173.

11. *Living*, 28.

12. Ibid.

13. *Living*, 111.

14. Ibid.

15. Charlotte Perkins Gilman Papers, Schlesinger Library, Radcliffe Institute, folder 36.

16. Gertrude Atherton, *Cosmopolitan*, 10 (Jan. 1891), 272.

17. Ambrose Bierce, "Prattle," *San Francisco Examiner*, Feb. 4, 1894, 6.

18. *The Diaries of Charlotte Perkins Gilman*, ed. Denise D. Knight (Charlottesville: Univ. Press of Virginia, 1994), 428. Hereafter, *Diaries.*

19. *Living*, 169.

20. *Diaries*, 472.

21. *Harper's Weekly*, Jan. 25, 1896, 79; Charlotte Perkins Gilman, "The New Poetry," *North American Review*, 168 (May 1899), 590.

22. Howells to Gilman, May 8, 1911, Gilman Papers, Schlesinger Library, Radcliffe Institute, folder 120.

23. Bellamy to Gilman, May 19, 1891, Gilman Papers, Schlesinger Library, Radcliffe Institute, folder 137.

24. Upton Sinclair, ed., *The Cry for Justice* (Philadelphia: Winston, 1915), 662.

25. Floyd Dell, *Women as World Builders: Studies in Modern Feminism* (Chicago: Forbes, 1913), 24.

26. *Bernard Shaw's Collected Letters 1898–1910*, ed. Dan H. Laurence (New York: Dodd, Mead, 1972), 346.

27. Lester Ward, *Glimpses of the Cosmos* (New York: Putnam's, 1917), vol. 5, 336–39.

28. *The Papers of Woodrow Wilson*, ed. Arthur S. Link (Princeton: Princeton Univ. Press, 1979), 22.

29. *Woman's Journal*, Feb. 1, 1896, 36.

30. "Mrs. Stetson as a Woman." *Topeka State Journal*, June 15, 1896, vol. 7.

31. *Endure: The Diaries of Charles Walter Stetson*, ed. Mary A. Hill (Philadelphia: Temple Univ. Press, 1985), 291.

32. Gilman Papers, Schlesinger Library, Radcliffe Institute, folder 259.

33. "Beginners," Charlotte Perkins Gilman Papers, Schlesinger Library, Radcliffe Institute, folder 165.

34. *Forerunner*, 2 (July 1911), 197. See also Joann P. Kreig, "Charlotte Perkins Gilman and the Whitman Connection," *Walt Whitman Quarterly Review*, 1 (Mar. 1984), 21–25.

35. *Amerikanische Turnzeitung*, Dec. 8, 1935, 9.

36. *Conservator*, 9 (Sept. 1898), 109.

37. Denise D. Knight, "'With the First Grass-Blade': Whitman's Influence on the Poetry of Charlotte Perkins Gilman," *Walt Whitman Quarterly Review*, 11 (Summer 1993), 19, 20.

38. Gilman wrote the remark on the manuscript copy of her poem, "Little Flutters of California Beauty." Gilman Papers, Schlesinger Library, Radcliffe Institute, folder 186.

39. Catherine J. Golden, "'Written to Drive Nails With': Recalling the Early Poetry of Charlotte Perkins Gilman." In *Charlotte Perkins Gilman: Optimist Reformer*, edited by Jill Rudd and Val Gough (Iowa City: Univ. of Iowa Press, 1999), 245, 246.

40. *The Man-Made World or, Our Androcentric Culture*, 3rd ed. (New York: Charlton, 1914), 24–25.

41. Emily Dickinson, [One Crucifixion is recorded—only—], *The Complete Poems of Emily Dickinson*, ed. Thomas H. Johnson (Boston: Little, Brown, 1960) 269.

**The World**

1. Clothes for an infant.

2. A mythological beast with multiple heads.

3. Gilman likens her attempts to revolutionize society to Columbus's voyage east by sailing west.

4. cuirass: a piece of armor that protects the breast and back.

5. "stiff-necked Jew": a stereotype of a Jewish zealot. From Exodus 32:9 in which God refers to the Jews as a "stiff-necked people" after some begin worshipping a golden calf.

6. Isaiah 53:3: "[Jesus was] despised and rejected of men; a man of sorrows, and acquainted with grief: and we hid as it were *our* faces from him; and he was despised, and we esteemed him not."

7. Exodus 20:12: "Thou shalt not murder. Thou shalt not commit adultery. Thou shalt not steal."

8. metempsychosis: transmigration of the soul.

9. Gilman refers to the prelapsarian period before the fall of Adam and Eve.

10. The teachings of Indian mystic Buddha (563?–483? BC) were rooted in the belief that humans could achieve perfect spiritual enlightenment.

11. Gilman refers to the biological imperative to reproduce.

12. English poet William Cowper (1731–1800) published the comic verse, "The Diverting History of John Gilpin," in 1785. The narrative poem traces the experience of a man who is taken for a ride by a runaway horse.

13. Plato (429–347 BC), Greek philosopher, author of *The Republic*.

14. helot: a serf.

15. Hebrews 12:6: "the Lord disciplines those he loves."

16. Romans 6:23: "For the wages of sin is death, but the gift of God is eternal life in Christ Jesus our Lord."

17. White Christ: The term was likely coined as a result of the white robes that newly converted Christians typically wore.

18. In Roman myth, Cupid is the god of erotic love, often represented with wings, bow, and quiver of arrows.

19. In Greek mythology, the nine Muses were goddesses who inspired artists, poets, philosophers, and musicians. The three Graces were goddesses of beauty, charm, and creativity.

20. Aphrodite was the Greek goddess of beauty and love.

21. simoon: a hot, sand-laden desert wind.

22. Tyre, Lebanon, the site of a flourishing maritime trade in ancient times, was conquered in 332 BC by Alexander the Great (356–323 BC), who gained control of the coastal region during the war between the Greeks and the Persians. Tyre eventually regained its independence and is today one of Lebanon's major seaports.

23. The world's third largest religion, Hinduism is characterized by a belief in reincarnation, karma, and by a desire for liberation from earthly evils. Hindu scriptures discuss such topics as theology, philosophy, and mythology and provide information about dharma, the practice of religious living.

24. In ancient times, Chaldea comprised a small plain in southern Babylonia that was formed by deposits from the Euphrates and Tigris rivers. The seers, or astrologers, charted the orbit of the planets to predict solar influences on events occurring on earth.

25. The site of several ancient civilzations, Assyria was centered on the Upper Tigris River in Mesopotamia, which is modern-day Iraq.

26. Exodus 15:4: "Pharaoh's chariots and his host hath he cast into the sea; his chosen captains are also drowned in the Red Sea."

27. The king of ancient Macedonia, Alexander the Great conquered the Persian Empire. He is regarded as one of the greatest warriors of all times. See note 20 above.

28. Persia was a theocratic Islamic republic in the Middle East in western Asia. Present-day Iran was the core of the ancient empire that was known as Persia until 1935.

29. Ethiops are natives of the African nation of Ethiopia, the Huns were a group of nomadic pastoral Asiatic people who invaded the Roman Empire in the fourth and fifth centuries AD.

30. In Germanic mythology, Thor was the god of thunder. His father, Odin, was regarded as the supreme god both in Germanic and Norse mythology.

31. Gilman commented in her autobiography that "The little 'Nevada Desert'" poem was returned to her by *Atlantic* editor Thomas Bailey Aldrich (1836–1907), who "remark[ed] that it needed the spot of color without which no picture was perfect. He had not seen Nevada" (*Living* 111).

32. In Greek myth, anyone who drinks from the River Lethe, one of the rivers of Hades, forgets everything.

33. The Powell-Mason cable car line in San Francisco opened in 1888. The cars still travel the route that Gilman describes.

34. The shopping, hotel, and theater district in downtown San Francisco is located around Union Square at Geary, Powell, Post, and Stockton streets.

35. Union Square: the heart of downtown San Francisco, named for the pro-Union rallies held there during the Civil War.

36. Gilman apparently refers to the gate to Chinatown just east of Powell Street.

37. Nob Hill is an exclusive, affluent neighborhood, originally named Nabob Hill, where such robber barons as Leland Stanford, Collis P. Huntington, and James Flood built mansions.

38. In Luke 16:19–31, Jesus narrates the parable of "The Rich Man and the Beggar Lazarus." In the Vulgate, or Latin, version of the text, the rich man is named Dives, Latin for "rich man."

39. The crest of Nob Hill is located near the intersection of Jones and Sacramento Streets.

40. Gilman contrasts the wealth on Nob Hill with the stench of the factory district "south of the slot," near where her journey began.

41. Russian Hill is north of Nob Hill, south of Fisherman's Wharf, and west of North Beach.

42. Mount Tamalpais is a 2,571-foot peak just north of the Golden Gate.

43. Angel Island, Treasure Island, and Alcatraz Island are in San Francisco Bay.

44. North Beach: a fashionable neighborhood in northeast San Francisco adjacent to Fisherman's Wharf.

45. Gilman is referring to the cities of Oakland and Berkeley.

46. Goat Island in San Francisco Bay, today renamed Yerba Buena Island.

47. Albion is the oldest known name for Great Britain.

48. The Pawtuxet River in Rhode Island, not far from Gilman's hometown of Providence.

49. The classical Romans associated roses with Venus, their name for the goddess of love.

50. Walt Whitman's *Leaves of Grass* (1855).

51. Daniel 1:5, 8: Nebuchadnezzar, the ruler of Babylon from 605 to 562 BC, appointed Daniel "a daily provision of the king's meat, and of the wine which he drank"; Daniel, however, "purposed in his heart that he would not defile himself with the portion of the king's meat, nor with the wine which he drank."

52. Eohippus: a small, five-toed ancestor of the horse that lived about 75 million years ago.

53. Dinoceras: a type of large prehistoric mammal vaguely resembling the rhinoceros.

54. Coryphodon: a type of large prehistoric mammal vaguely resembling the hippopotamus.

55. Psychozoic: designating or applying to the era of man.

56. Now known as *Eobasileus cornutus*, *Loxolophodon cornutus* was a plant-eating, rhinoceros-like, hoofed mammal.

57. The Eocene era, which existed about a million years ago, is a major division of the geologic timescale and the second epoch of the Palaeogene period in the Cenozoic era.

58. Native to Eurasia and North America some four million years ago, mastodons resembled woolly mammoths and modern elephants.

59. Neolithic Man lived 10,000–3,500 BC.

60. The most famous work of rock art at the time Gilman wrote this poem was an engraving of a mammoth on a fragment of mammoth ivory discovered by Edouard Lartet in 1864 in the La Madeleine cave in France. It was exhibited at the Grand Exposition Universelle in Paris in 1867 and featured in Charles Lyell's *The Geological Evidences of the Antiquity of Man* (1873). According to Frederick Starr ("Some Early Homes of Mankind: The Cave-Dwellers," *Arthur's Home Magazine*, 63 [1893], 708), only two other prehistoric drawings or engravings of mammoths had been discovered by 1893.

61. There is evidence that Gilman continued to revise "A Conservative" some time after its initial publication. Among the Gilman papers that are still owned by her grandson is an intriguing three-stanza addendum to the poem, written in Gilman's hand and titled "Supplement to 'A Conservative.'" The addendum reads as follows:

> I saw, and this was quite as strange,
>> I saw a half-blind man
> Fold down the creature's gauzy wings
>> As ladies fold a fan;
>
> And then, with careful, tender stroke,
>> Now that way and now this,
> He drew about the shuddering form
>> The broken chrysalis,
>
> And gently held it thus and prayed,
>> At every painful squirm,
> "God grant your wishes, little dear,
>> Go back and be a worm!"

62. A biblical figure renowned for his wisdom; e.g., "The whole world sought audience with Solomon to hear the wisdom God had put in his heart." (1 Kings 10:24)

63. The granite obelisk monument commemorating the Revolutionary War battle on Bunker Hill on June 17, 1775, was dedicated in 1843.

64. "fox who lost his tail": an Aesop's fable.

65. pastellette: a splash of color.

66. Jesus' parable in Matthew 13:45–46: "the kingdom of heaven is like unto a merchant man, seeking goodly pearls: Who, when he had found one pearl of great price, went and sold all that he had, and bought it.

67. In this poem "unmentionable" refers to expectoration, or spitting.

68. "weather-breeder": A New England expression for a pleasant day that precedes a storm.

## Woman

1. That is, man and woman.

2. According to Genesis 2:9 and 2:16–17, Adam and Eve were forbidden to eat from the Tree of Knowledge in Eden.

3. Lady Macbeth to her husband (I, 5: 16–18): "I do fear thy nature; / It is too full o' th' milk of human kindness."

4. Gilman also quoted this English proverb in chapter 3 of *Women and Economics*.

5. Genesis 3:17, God says to Adam: "Because you have heeded the voice of your wife, and have eaten from the tree of which I commanded you, saying, 'You shall not eat of it': Cursed *is* the ground for your sake; In toil you shall eat *of* it all the days of your life."

6. According to the Book of Genesis, Eve was created by God from Adam's rib. After succumbing to the serpent's suggestion that she eat the forbidden fruit from the Tree of Knowledge, God cast her and Adam out of the Garden of Eden.

7. In Greek mythology, Pandora was a perfect and beautiful woman married to Epimetheus. Instructed by Zeus not to open a box that she had been given, Pandora's curiosity led her to open it, thereby releasing all of evils that mankind had not previously known.

8. In Greek mythology, Hercules was the son of Zeus and was renowned for his strength.

9. According to Christian mythology, the Holy Grail, a chalice with miraculous powers, was used by Jesus at the Last Supper.

10. New England farmhouses were often designed in the shape of an "L," with the part devoted to labor (kitchen, pantry, etc.) perpendicular to the parlor and bedrooms.

11. scolding bridles: a British invention made of iron to gag women who gossiped and quarreled.

12. ducking stools: a form of medieval water torture usually used against women.

13. Gilman's verse is a parody of Whitman's "The Dalliance of Eagles."

14. "Mother's Doughnuts": a popular dialect poem by Charles Fallon Adams first published in *Harper's Monthly* for June 1885.

15. The reference to mother's knees is a familiar one and has been used by such authors as Charlotte Brontë in her poem "The Missionary" (1846) and by John Greenleaf Whittier in "The Human Sacrifice" (1843).

16. hod: a coal scuttle.

17. Gilman's note.

18. French heels: high-heeled shoes.

19. Mr. Punch was an anarchic trickster figure, often represented in the Punch and Judy puppet show or on the masthead of the British humor magazine *Punch*.

20. New Woman: a suffragist or feminist who sought social, economic, and academic equality, as opposed to the True Woman, who was content with the socially prescribed roles of wife and mother.

21. divided skirt: a dress pattern for women that permitted cross-saddle horseback riding and other sports.

22. Blue Book: a social registry of elite or wealthy members of a community.

23. The day of the week a genteel woman received visitors.

24. worker bee: a female bee that is unable to reproduce.

25. Gilman discusses her theory of racial progress throughout *Women and Economics*. Her racism and support of social purity and eugenics are well documented.

## The March

1. The wolf at the door is used both as a metaphor for one who is predatory and for creditors who come to collect debts. Keeping the wolf from the door also refers to attempting to avoid poverty or starvation.

2. Rouge et Noir: literally "red and black," a solitaire card game.

3. Gilman's note. L. L. Polk (1837–1892), the president of the National Farmers' Alliance, gave a speech on April 11, 1890, before the Senate Committee on Agriculture and Forestry in Kansas City, Missouri. Polk referred to "the universal wail of hard times and distress" and noted that "the farmer sows in faith, he toils in hope, but reaps in disappointment and despair." An article by the Associated Press mocked the talk.

4. See "The World," note 38, above.

5. Abel and Cain: the sons of Adam and Eve whose story is told in Genesis 4:1–16. Cain, a farmer, murders Abel, a shepherd.

6. Gilman revises Paul's injunction: "If a man will not work, he shall not eat" (II Thessalonians 3:10).

7. William Shakespeare (1564–1616), English playwright and poet. Gilman read at least twenty-one of Shakespeare's plays.

8. Homer (ca. eighth century BC), Greek epic poet.

9. Socrates (469–399 BC), Greek philosopher.

10. Richard Wagner (1813–83), German operatic composer.

11. Ludwig van Beethoven (1712–73), German composer and pianist.

12. Johann Sebastian Bach (1685–1750), German composer and organist.

13. Benjamin Franklin (1706–90), American statesman, scientist, and inventor.

14. Samuel F. B. Morse (1791–1872), inventor of the single-wire telegraph.

15. Thomas Alva Edison (1847–1931), inventor of the electric light and phonograph.

16. James Watt (1736–1819) invented the steam engine in 1769.

17. George Stephenson (1781–1848), inventor of the first steam locomotive engine.

18. Alexander Graham Bell (1847–1922), inventor of the telephone.

19. Euclid (ca. third century BC), Greek mathematician, often thought to be inventor of geometry.

20. Aristotle (384–322 BC), Greek philosopher.

21. Michelangelo (1475–1564), Italian Renaissance painter and sculptor.

22. Christopher Columbus (1451–1506), Italian explorer.

23. Sir Walter Raleigh (1554?–1618), English soldier and explorer.

24. George Washington (1732–99), commander-in-chief of the Continental Army during the American Revolution and the first president of the United States.

25. palace car: a deluxe railroad train manufactured by the Pullman Company of Chicago that included plush seating, artwork on the walls, and other amenities not usually found in train travel in its day.

26. Nationalism was a form of Christian socialism inspired by the utopian novel *Looking Backward 1887–2000* by Edward Bellamy (1850–1898). Gilman began her professional career as a Nationalist lecturer and poet.

27. Jeremiah, the so-called broken-hearted prophet of the Hebrew Bible, whose writings were punctuated with lamentation and warning.

28. goose that laid the golden egg: an Aesop's fable.

29. "Farmer's Ring": An allusion to the organized farm movement, including the Grange. See note 3 above in "The March."

30. Isaac Watts (1674–1748) was a theologian and founder of English hymnody.

31. See notes 3 and 29 above.

32. Amœboids (amoebas) are life-forms composed of only one cell that has no fixed shape.

33. "survival of the fittest": a phrase coined by Herbert Spencer in *Principles of Biology* (1864).

34. Crœsus, also known as Cresus, (560–546) was the last king of Lydia. His kingdom, which had prospered during his reign, fell to the Persians under Cyrus.

35. In Acts 20:35 the apostle Paul quotes Jesus: "It is more blessed to give than to receive."

36. bedizen: to dress in a gaudy manner.

### Uncollected and Other Poems

1. Gilman's note.

2. mere: a small marsh or pond.

3. the Roman Catholic Church.

4. The Unitarian minister Edward Everett Hale (1822–1909) was a social reformer and a prolific writer, best remembered today for his tale "The Man Without a Country" (1863). He was Gilman's uncle.

5. Gilman's note.

6. Genesis 9: 20–21: Noah, a man of the soil, began to plant a vineyard. When he drank some of the wine, he got drunk and uncovered himself inside his tent.

7. *Chevaix-de-frise*: portable military barricades typically made of wood or stone. They were used in earlier times to block approaching armies.

8. Gilman's note. The poem is a scathing indictment of John D. Rockefeller (1839–1937).

9. virgin's lamp: see Jesus' Parable of the Ten Virgins (Matthew 25:1–13).

10. widow's cruse: I Kings 17:8–16.

11. Luke 18:22: "Now when Jesus heard these things, he said unto him, 'Yet lackest thou one thing: sell all that thou hast, and distribute unto the poor, and thou shalt have treasure in heaven: and come, follow me.'"

12. The so-called oil trust, led by Rockefeller's Standard Oil Company, allegedly sold oil in the export market for less than the price of oil in the U.S. market.

13. Matthew 16:24: "Then said Jesus unto his disciples, If any man will come after me, let him deny himself, and take up his cross, and follow me."

14. In John 12:8, Jesus says, "For the poor always ye have with you; but me ye have not always."

15. Matthew 15:14: "Let them alone: they be blind leaders of the blind. And if the blind lead the blind, both shall fall into the ditch.

16. Gilman apparently refers to the Molly Maguires, mostly Irish miners in the anthracite coal region of Pennsylvania, who organized the Workingmen's Benevolent Association to protest unsafe working conditions, child labor, and low wages in the 1870s without much success.

17. Gilman occasionally quoted Emerson in her letters and diaries, as in her August 1, 1881, letter to longtime friend Martha Luther Lane, where she wrote, "I read Emersons incomprehensible conundrum! My mind was his for a moment! . . . I shan't write an [*sic*] more Sage just now, this whole essay is alive, and I can't wait till you return to read it to you."

18. Gilman's revision of Isaiah 9:6: "To us a child is born; to us a son is given."

19. A term coined by Charles Henry Parkhurst (1842–1933) to mean the "passionate aping of everything that is mannish." See "Calls Them Andromaniacs," *New York Times*, 23 May 1897, p. 16.

20. London-born John Burns (1858–1943) was an engineer who became outraged by the treatment of Africans when he went to work for the United Africa Company. Convinced that socialism would remove the disparities between races and classes, he founded the Social Democratic Federation, which he later left. He was a leader of the London Dock Strike, lobbying on behalf of the dockworkers and raising large sums of money from various trade unions to help the strikers.

21. See note 12 above.

22. Gilman visited the Ruskin Colony in Ruskin, Tennessee, in 1898. A utopian socialist community founded in 1894 by newspaper editor Julius Augustus Wayland, the colony was named after English socialist writer John Ruskin. Its members sought to establish a number of rural socialist settlements founded on a cooperative commonwealth. In her autobiography, Gilman denounced the colony as a product of a "high-minded idioc[y]" that "overlook[ed] the necessity for a legitimate local economic base" and whose members "are of the sort who need to be taken care of, not world-builders at all" (*Living* 252–53). During her visit, Gilman stayed in a rat-infested cabin, an experience that prompted the verse.

23. Elizabeth Cady Stanton (1815–1902) was an abolitionist and leader of the nineteenth-century women's movement. She organized the 1848 Women's Rights Convention in

Seneca Falls, New York, and was author of the historic "Declaration of Sentiments," a document listing a number of grievances suffered by women and proposing social reforms that would promote equal rights. In 1895, Stanton published *The Woman's Bible*.

24. Cornelia Collins Hussey (1827–1902) was a suffragist and founder of the New York Infirmary for Women and Children. She was a member of the Women's Christian Temperance Union and vice-president of the National Woman's Suffrage Society.

25. In Greek mythology, Danae was a beautiful princess whose father Acrisius locked her away in a bronze tower after being told by a prophet that Danae would bear a son who would eventually kill him. After Zeus fell in love with her, he transformed himself into a shower of gold that poured from the tower ceiling and onto her lap, causing her to be impregnated with Zeus's child.

26. An allusion to canto 56 of Tennyson's "In Memoriam": "Nature, red in tooth and claw."

27. American dramatist Clyde Fitch (1865–1909) wrote the lyrics to a popular song "Love Makes The World Go 'Round" (1896) with an arrangement by William Furst.

28. See note 22 of "The March," above.

29. English naturalist Charles Darwin (1809–1882) proposed the theory of natural selection, which became the cornerstone of evolutionary thought. His most influential books were *On the Origin of the Species by Means of Natural Selection* (1859) and *The Descent of Man* (1871). Coined in the late nineteenth century, the term Social Darwinism advanced the idea that humans compete in a struggle for existence in which natural selection results in survival of the fittest. Gilman's *Women and Economics* is based on the theory that female subjugation is an unnatural consequence of women's economic dependence on men.

30. German educator Friedrich Wilhelm August Fröbel (1782–1852) created the concept of kindergarten and advocated for activity-based education.

31. See note 16, in "The March" above.

32. Hindustan: northern India.

33. *What Diantha Did*, originally serialized in *The Forerunner* in 1909–10, traces the ascent of an enterprising young woman who professionalizes housekeeping and food services to free women from the household drudgery, which, according to Gilman in such works as *Women and Economics* and *The Home*, needlessly imprisoned them in the domestic sphere.

34. *The Crux*, originally serialized in *The Forerunner* in 1911, tells the story of a young New England woman who breaks her engagement and flees west to Colorado after learning that her fiancé has syphilis. The novel argues not only for women's sexual self-determination, but it also makes a case for many of the social reforms that Gilman advocated, including economic self-sufficiency and professionalized child care and housekeeping.

35. Air: Kathleen Aroon: to be sung to the tune of "Kathleen Aroon," by German composer Franz Abt (1819–1885).

36. Journalist and author Alexander Black (1859–1940) and his wife, Elizabeth, were longtime friends of Gilman's.

37. Gilman's math seems in error here. U.S. defense spending in 1934 amounted to about $1.1 billion and total federal spending to about $5.9 billion.

38. The Ninth Conference on the Cause and Cure of War was held in Washington, D.C., 16–19 January 1934. Founded in 1924 by Carrie Chapman Catt (1859–1947), the conference promoted the position that "the peace movement is less to overcome outspoken and convinced opposition than to arouse inert masses of people to a sense of responsibility for the elimination of war."

39. Amelia, Latin for industrious or beloved, was Gilman's nickname for long-time friend Grace Ellery Channing (1862–1937). Sophie, Latin for wisdom and knowledge, is an abbreviation for Sophronia, the nickname Gilman adopted for herself in various letters to Channing.

40. To be sung to the tune of "The Battle Hymn of the Republic."

41. David Hume (1711–1776) was a Scottish economist, historian, and a philosophical empiricist and religious skeptic.

42. Gilman burlesques solipsism or the philosophical idea that nothing outside the individual mind can be proven to exist.

# WORKS CITED

*Amerikanische Turnzeitung,* Dec. 8, 1935, 9.

Atherton, Gertrude, *Cosmopolitan* 10 (Jan. 1891): 272.

Bellamy, Edward. Letter to Gilman, Feb. 19, 1891. Gilman Papers, Schlesinger Library, Radcliffe Institute, folder 120.

———. *Looking Backward 2000–1887.* Boston: Ticknor and Company, 1888.

Bierce, Ambrose. "Prattle." *San Francisco Examiner,* Feb. 4, 1894, 6.

Caesar, Julius. *Caesar's Commentaries: On the Gallic War and On the Civil War.* Edited by James H. Ford and translated by W. A. MacDevitt. El Paso: El Paso Norte Press, 2005.

Dell, Floyd. *Women as World Builders: Studies in Modern Feminism.* Chicago: Forbes, 1913.

Dickinson, Emily. ["One Crucifixion is recorded—only—"], *The Complete Poems of Emily Dickinson.* Edited by Thomas H. Johnson. Boston: Little, Brown, 1960. 269.

———. ["The Book of Martyrs"], *The Poems of Emily Dickinson.* Edited by Mabel Loomis Todd and Thomas Wentworth Higginson. Boston: Robert Brothers, 1890. 32.

Gilman, Charlotte Perkins. "The Answer." *Woman's Journal,* Oct. 2, 1886, 313.

———. "Beginners." Gilman Papers, Schlesinger Library, Radcliffe Institute, folder 165.

———. *The Crux.* New York: Charlton, 1911.

———. The *Diaries of Charlotte Perkins Gilman.* 2 vols. Edited by Denise D. Knight. Charlottesville: Univ. Press of Virginia, 1994.

———. "The Duty Farthest." *Impress,* Nov. 17, 1894, 4.

———. *Forerunner* 1–7 (1909–1916). Reprint. New York: Greenwood, 1968.

———. *His Religion and Hers.* New York: Century, 1923.

———. *The Home.* New York: McClure, Phillips & Co., 1903.

———. "In Duty Bound." *Woman's Journal,* Jan. 12, 1884, 14.

———. *In This Our World.* 1893. 3rd ed. Boston: Small, Maynard, 1898.

———. *The Later Poetry of Charlotte Perkins Gilman.* Edited Denise D. Knight. Newark: Univ. of Delaware Press, 1996.

———. *The Living of Charlotte Perkins Gilman: An Autobiography.* New York: Appleton-Century, 1935. Madison: Univ. of Wisconsin Press, 1990.

———. *The Man-Made World or, Our Androcentric Culture,* 3rd ed. New York: Charlton, 1914.

———. "Similar Cases." *Nationalist,* 2 (April 1890), 165–66.

———. *What Diantha Did.* New York: Charlton, 1910.

———. *Women and Economics: A Study of the Economic Relation between Men and Women as a Factor in Social Evolution.* Boston: Small, Maynard, 1898.

Golden, Catherine J. "'Written to Drive Nails With': Recalling the Early Poetry of Charlotte Perkins Gilman." In *Charlotte Perkins Gilman: Optimist Reformer,* edited by Jill Rudd and Val Gough, 243–66. Iowa City: Univ. of Iowa Press, 1999.

Hale, Edward Everett. "The Man without a Country." Boston: Ticknor and Fields, 1863.

Howells, William Dean. Letter to Gilman, May 8, 1911. Gilman Papers, Schlesinger Library, Radcliffe Institute, folder 120.

———. Review of *In This Our World,* 2nd ed. *Harper's Weekly* (Jan. 24, 1896): 79.

———. Review of *In This Our World,* 3rd ed. *North American Review* 168 (May 1899): 590.

Knight, Denise D. "'With the First Grass-Blade': Whitman's Influence on the Poetry of Charlotte Perkins Gilman." *Walt Whitman Quarterly Review* 11 (Summer 1993): 18–29.

Kreig, Joann P. "Charlotte Perkins Gilman and the Whitman Connection." *Walt Whitman Quarterly Review,* 1 (March 1984): 21–25.

"Mrs. Stetson as a Woman." *Topeka State Journal* 7 (June 15, 1896).

Shaw, Bernard. *Bernard Shaw's Collected Letters 1898–1910.* Edited by Dan H. Laurence. New York: Dodd, Mead, 1972.

Sinclair, Upton, ed. *The Cry for Justice.* Philadelphia: Winston, 1915.

Steinbeck, John. *The Grapes of Wrath.* New York: Viking, 1939.

Stetson, Charles Walter. *Endure: The Diaries of Charles Walter Stetson.* Edited by Mary A. Hill. Philadelphia: Temple Univ. Press, 1985.

Traubel, Horace. Review of *In This Our World,* 3rd ed. *Conservator,* 9 (Sept. 1898): 109.

Ward, Lester. *Glimpses of the Cosmos.* New York: Putnam's, 1917.

Wilson, Woodrow. *The Papers of Woodrow Wilson.* Edited by Arthur S. Link. Princeton: Princeton Univ. Press, 1979.

Whitman, Walt. *Leaves of Grass.* 1855. Boston: James R. Osgood, 1881.

*Woman's Journal* (Feb. 1, 1896): 36.